NO MORE "US" AND "THEM"

Classroom Lessons and Activities to Promote Peer Respect

Lesley Roessing

ROWMAN & LITTLEFIELD EDUCATION

A division of
ROWMAN & LITTLEFIELD PUBLISHERS, INC.
Lanham • New York • Toronto • Plymouth, UK

Description of the Home Front Fair activity was included with permission of the Association of Middle Level Education. www.amle.org

Lesley Roessing, "Building a Community of Stories and Writers: Lake Wobegon Comes to the Classroom." *The Quarterly of the National Writing Project* 26, 4 (2004). www.nwp.org/cs/public/print/resource/2147. Copyright 2004, National Writing Project. Reprinted with Permission.

Published by Rowman & Littlefield Education
A division of Rowman & Littlefield Publishers, Inc.
A wholly owned subsidiary of
The Rowman & Littlefield Publishing Group, Inc.
4501 Forbes Boulevard, Suite 200, Lanham, Maryland 20706
www.rowman.com

10 Thornbury Road, Plymouth PL6 7PP, United Kingdom

British Library Cataloguing in Publication Information Available

Library of Congress Cataloging-in-Publication Data

Roessing, Lesley.
  No more "us" and "them" : classroom lessons and activities to promote peer respect / Lesley Roessing.
      pages cm
  Includes bibliographical references.
  ISBN 978-1-61048-812-9 (cloth : alk. paper) — ISBN 978-1-61048-813-6 (pbk. : alk. paper) — ISBN 978-1-61048-814-3 (electronic)
  1. Interaction analysis in education. 2. Communication in education. 3. Active learning. I. Title.
  LB1034.R64 2012
  371.102'2—dc23

                                                                    2012003720

Printed in the United States of America

For Dean, my grandson,
and a future in which he and his classmates
will work together in an atmosphere of mutual respect.

CONTENTS

LIST OF ACTIVITIES AND LESSONS BY CHAPTER

FOREWORD

I loved reading this book . . . and you will, too! As a former middle school language arts teacher, I was grabbed by *No More "Us" and "Them"* and pulled right back into a middle school classroom. It is evident from reading this book that author Lesley Roessing was an outstanding middle school teacher. She knows her students well, she understands how young adolescents learn and what they should learn, and she certainly knows how to motivate students and get them to understand each other. But you will know all of that before you even hit chapter 1.

What I liked best about *No More "Us" and "Them"* is the clear focus on students, learning about each other and learning to understand, respect, and get along with each other. Talk about twenty-first-century skills! Words like *respect, tolerance, acceptance*, and *diversity* show that Roessing has a firm grasp on the needs of her young adolescent clientele.

In this era where STEM programs—science, technology, engineering, and mathematics—are at the top of the heap, it is refreshing to read about such an excellent example of humanities, language arts, and social studies programs in which students grapple with the issues they will deal with the rest of their lives and in which, in the context of a high-level curriculum, students meet essential standards.

This engaging book takes us through an entire year with Roessing, her middle school students, and other teachers and students with whom she has worked, as they explore the themes of tolerance and acceptance, diversity and understanding, respect and selflessness, collaboration and interdependence. Each chapter represents another section of the year and sets out broad curriculum goals with specific examples of individual and group projects; with descriptions of how the projects worked in classrooms in rural, suburban, and urban areas of the country; and with tons of resources to use in your classroom.

At the beginning of the year, Roessing asked students to write "I Am" poems to get to know each other; they also took part in many activities by which they gently learned about the differences and similarities of students who fascinated them. A bit later, the "Poetry in Two Voices" and "Where I Am From" poems allowed students to explore who they are and what they bring to the classroom. Excellent examples of activities for different content areas, such as math, science, foreign language, and music classes, are also given here and throughout the book.

In chapter 3, "Becoming Part of the Puzzle," Roessing demonstrates the power of diversity through class metaphors. A metaphor for a class, the class as an orchestra, with everyone adding a different piece of the music, was a powerful way for students to see their value as individuals and as part of the larger group of students. Then students devised their own metaphors for America and the American people, all the while discussing and studying the value of diversity. Certainly, a powerful chapter for young adolescents as they find their way in this world.

Through a study of contemporary fiction and nonfiction, including a variety of genres such as novels, short stories, poetry, magazine stories, games, and much more, students explore the concept of "everyone as an expert," with which they identify and appreciate their areas of expertise by completing surveys and discussing their individual strengths, interests, travels, families, and more. I liked this chapter because it illustrated a number of ways to teach our students how to value their strengths. Too often young adolescents deal with each other on superficial levels, paying attention to such things as clothing, attitude, and possessions, the kinds of things they see valued in the media, rather than the internal and interesting qualities of a person that really matter.

Also, students learned to see themselves as experts in a variety of areas as the author/teacher stressed authentic collaboration, not just working with classmates, but also working with a classmates who genuinely had something to share because of their expertise in a particular area. Grammar gurus, website wonders, knowing-when-to-spellcheck whizzes, and proofreading prodigies were just some of the class experts. Young adolescents have much to share, and this book shows how to make that critical collaboration happen.

One of the key themes of *No More "Us" and "Them"* is the distinction between a person being "different" from someone else—and recognizing that difference as worthy—versus the more typical young adolescent designation "weird" to note difference and most likely disapproval. How does one overcome this tendency to dismiss others and judge them as inferior? Simple? Hardly. Roessing suggests that teachers must focus on similarities and acknowledge the value of diversity, even as students are learning about themselves, while studying many other cultures beyond their own small communities.

In chapter 6, there are many ideas to move well beyond a single multicultural event—day, week, or month—to learn about other cultures, with the focus on students becoming "them" . . . and part of the class. Roessing makes a strong case for including the study of culture an integral part of the curriculum, instead of celebrating a particular event once every year. Lots of excellent examples are given, such as celebrating a Human Rights Leader's Day. A fully drawn unit describes a cultural study using the Cinderella fairy tale: "By presenting authentic information about the geography, environment, government family structure, food, clothing, class system, rituals, and values of a culture, folktales help children better understand cultures of diverse times and places, acknowledge their interrelatedness, and develop an appreciation for the customs and beliefs or different peoples."

Here is an inside tip: read chapter 9 twice, once as you begin the book to find out how this approach works and then again as you complete the book to truly understand how it all works. In a series of excellent examples in a variety of different content areas, Roessing takes students one step beyond acceptance and value to respect.

In addition to the excellent rationale for teaching young adolescents to learn tolerance, understanding, and respect, and the many examples of using literature and incorporating reading and writing across the curriculum, this book is filled with lists of books and other resources that support these critical themes. In chapter 8, for example, Roessing lists loads and loads of references—picture books, short story and poetry collections, novels, memoirs, magazines, and all types of nonfiction as well. These references by themselves are worth the price of this book!

Every middle school teacher should read *No More "Us" and "Them"* to see how teachers can help students through self-discovery-style personal learning and, ultimately, to respect for every individual. This is real life, and it is elegantly presented here for teachers of every subject.

In this book, every student's journey is inspirational as each struggles with what it means to be a human being. This is a journey that every young adolescent and their teachers must undertake together.

Dr. Edward N. Brazee
professor emeritus of education, University of Maine
former editor of professional publications,
Association for Middle Level Education

ACKNOWLEDGMENTS

As they say, "it takes a village . . ." and I want to thank those members of my village who helped make writing and publishing this book possible:

- my Ridley Middle School principals Richard Cunningham, Gail Heinemeyer, and Chas Maiers, who allowed me the autonomy to create a curriculum that addressed the standards but also prepared my students as citizens of their classroom, team, school, and their future worlds;
- my Ridley Raiders Team colleagues—Tony, Joyce, Patricia, Steve, Beth, Frau, and others—who supported and many times joined in on the activities and lessons in this book;
- the teachers who have invited me into their classrooms and shared their students with me;
- the teachers who implemented ideas, activities, and lessons discovered thorough my articles, workshops, or conference presentations and then shared their results with me;
- Judith Garrison, AASU head reference librarian, who helped my through the twenty-first-century citation challenge;
- Armstrong student Giovanni Wyatt, who shared the Fave graph and chart activity that was part of her project for our class on diversity education;

Armstrong COE Dean Pat Wachholz, who has supported my publications and provided an ongoing sounding board for my ideas;

Ed Brazee, who offered his support and wrote such a kind, thoughtful, and thorough, foreword;

Carla Weiland, Pat George, and other AMLE staff, editors, and colleagues who know and share with others the importance of teaching the child and have helped me reach teachers with that message;

my family—husband Chuck, Meg, Matt, and Julia—who listen to me rattle on about ideas I want to try and write about and help me find the "perfect word," and my parents who raised me to think beyond tolerance to respect; and

Tom Koerner and Mary McMenamin, and the many other staff members of Rowman & Littlefield Education, who have made working on this book such a pleasurable experience.

INTRODUCTION

It's the beginning of May. We are writing memoirs in language arts class and holding an old-fashioned show-and-tell, something these adolescents have not experienced since the self-confident days of kindergarten. Several girls have baby blankets and stuffed animals. Not surprising. But so do some of the boys.

Many students have artifacts from distant countries and cultures and religions. Heidi has her grandmother's Star of David necklace, and Rashid has a chain he will explain to his group. Candace's family lost most of their possessions in a fire the past year, but she brings the key to her former home. The students sit in random groups as they arrive. It doesn't appear to matter with whom they sit as they grab the nearest available seat.

At that first show-and-tell, I looked around in amazement, surprised that these adolescents felt safe enough with each other to share artifacts of their personal pasts, their families' pasts, their cultures, their religions, their histories, and their varied circumstances. But maybe I should not have been so surprised; this was what I had been working towards all year.

I taught two different language arts courses: in some classes we studied language arts; in others we studied humanities, a blend of language arts and social studies centered around a theme of social justice. Certainly we had curriculum and state standards to cover, but, in both courses, I guided the curriculum toward a study of tolerance and acceptance and implemented strategies and cooperative, collaborative groupings that had led us to this moment.

In *Us and Them: Understanding Your Tribal Mind*, David Berreby maintains that "organizing other humans into kinds . . . is the mind's guide for understanding anyone we don't know personally, for seeing our place in the human world, and for judging our actions." He further contends that there is "'apparently no people known to history or anthropology that lacks a distinction between "us" and "others,"' and particularly others who don't rise to our level" (Romano 2011, B5).

There is actually a modern verb for that concept: "otherize," which the Urban Dictionary defines as "to make into the 'other' to separate from the 'our.'"

Hearing the term used matter-of-factly in a news report recently, I began to reflect on my middle grade classroom and about what steps I take, or what steps educators can take, to create an atmosphere where adolescent students feel accepted, included, and valuable to themselves and to their peers.

The goal of this book is not to present a study of prejudice and discrimination but to change adolescent attitudes to lead not just to acceptance and tolerance but toward an expansion of "us" and respect for their classmates. Hopefully, that will spread an even wider net of respect.

This feeling of community is especially important in the middle grades where the most bullying takes place. A study conducted by the Youth Voice Project, the first known large-scale research project that solicited students' perceptions about strategy effectiveness to reduce peer mistreatment in our schools, reports that "the majority of traumatized students were in grades 6–8."

Students reported in this survey that accessing support from peers and adults was the most helpful strategy to "make things better." Focusing on the facet of support from peers, the two strategies reported as most effective in making things better were when peers "spent time with me" and "talked to me," both acts of alliance.

A preliminary conclusion from the data suggests, "Our students report that asking for and getting emotional support and a sense of connection has helped them the most among all the strategies we compared." Conversely, "Peers were reported as being able to have a significant negative effect by blaming or making fun of mistreated youth."

In "The 'In' Crowd and Social Cruelty" (2002), an ABC News Special on bullying, Wendy Craig, a Queen's University professor of psychology, explained the power of peer support to reporter John Stossel. "If one child says, 'Stop it,' it will end the bullying within ten seconds."

Therefore, it is imperative that teachers build community in their classrooms and across their academic teams and grades to make school a safe and supportive place for adolescents. It is also essential that teachers help their students acknowledge that they belong to a group together, that they are part of a "we" or "us," and that any differences—divergent talents, backgrounds, experiences, and skills—only make *us* stronger and better.

Barbara Coloroso (2011, 52), educator and author of several books on bullying, explains the connection between lack of respect and bullying: "Contrary to popular opinion and contrary to the thesis of some anti-bullying programs, bullying is not about anger or conflict. It's about contempt—a powerful feeling of dislike towards someone considered to be worthless, inferior or undeserving of respect. Bullying is arrogance in action. Once kids believe that someone is 'less than them' they can harm that child without feeling any empathy, compassion or shame."

We start with seeing similarities. People are more comfortable with those with whom they share likenesses. Therefore, the first step is for adolescents to discover what they have in common, seeing the similarities among themselves. This is much easier for younger children than for adolescents. "Young children will play contentedly together whatever their race or national origin"; thus, "prejudice is not inborn but acquired" (Allport 1976, 517).

According to Beverly Daniel Tatum, author of *Why Are All the Black Kids Sitting Together in the Cafeteria?* "We have all gotten misinformation about people who are different from ourselves. It doesn't really matter where you grew up. You've been exposed to stereotypes about groups other than your own, and to some extent, your own group." She explains why students sit together: "Sometimes, people are together because of shared experiences" (Mask and George 2004).

However, seeing similarities is only the first step. Lois Lowry's futuristic novel *The Giver* (1993), a novel read widely in middle-level classes, illustrates both the advantages and disadvantages of sameness.

Sameness is not always a virtue. Teachers need to ensure that students take a second step—appreciating the differences among themselves, valuing diversity. Taught to work cooperatively, students will usually find the more varied a group, the more it can accomplish and the richer the collaboration. This realization grows as a result of progression from seeing sameness to valuing diversity.

In *Reducing Prejudice and Discrimination,* Johnson and Johnson (2000, 241) pointed out that schools may be the one place where diverse adolescents are together for significant periods of time, and, therefore, educators have unique opportunities to encourage interactions and relationships that decrease stereotyping and prejudice by creating a cooperative community and positive interdependence. "Positive interdependence may be structured through mutual goals, joint rewards, shared resources, complementary roles, division of labor, and a mutual identity."

Even though many neighborhoods are becoming more diverse, this is still true. School may be the one place where diverse adolescents work together and hear each other's voices.

In "Living on the Edge: Confronting Social Injustices," Marshall George (2002, 39) writes that after walking the streets of New York on September 11, 2001, he "was even more convinced that we educators must take responsibility for putting a stop to the hatred for and disenfranchisement of those whom we see as being different from us."

George suggests that teachers accomplish this through integrating adolescent literature and expository texts into their language arts and social studies curriculum, although activities, assignments, and projects, and even young adult literature, can be integrated into all classes.

However, teachers and preservice teachers constantly worry about adding anything to their plate. They talk about curriculum, standards, pacing guides, and preparing for standardized tests. This book endeavors to outline ideas for strategies and activities that can be integrated into existing curricula and in lessons that meet curricular standards.

Examples of strategies, projects, and activities that I integrated into my own language arts and humanities curricula and in classes I visited and observed are incorporated. In some cases, detailed lesson plans are described. Ideas and adaptations for other content areas—social studies, science, mathematics, foreign languages, physical education and health, art, music, as well as advisory or homeroom periods and team activities and gatherings—are proposed to expand our students' circle of "us," to build community in our classrooms, our academic teams, and our schools. The aspiration is to make each of our students value each other and feel respected as a piece of the puzzle.

Several activities facilitate adolescents in becoming acquainted and forming relationships with one another, and many will help students to see the similarities that are not always visible. Other activities and actions facilitate awareness of the value of diversity among peers. Yet other events and assignments will empower students as they begin to appreciate themselves as experts and, therefore, as of special importance to the classroom community as a collaborative entity.

In several chapters, I also propose literary texts that can supplement activities and the affective lessons to be drawn from them. The activities and readings are developmentally responsive and can be used in conjunction with classroom lessons or implemented independently to create equity in a classroom community, stimulate classroom discussion, and lead to challenging assignments. A community is built cumulatively, one activity at a time.

❶

GETTING TO KNOW YOU

It's the first day of school. Teachers look around the room. Strangers all. Students look around the room. Some spot friends and sit down by them. They warily look at the *others*, leaving them out of conversations.

"Who are they?" their teacher thinks. "How will I get to know them?"

"Who are *they*?" each student thinks. "How will I get to know *them*? How will *they* get to know me?"

In their school uniforms or teenage fashions, during those first days, all students look pretty much alike. Teachers know that at some point they will learn their students' names and be able to tell them apart, but how will each teacher get to know them, who they are? It is even more important that teachers help them to forge new friendships, to make each class *us*, not "us" and "them."

First, teachers learn the names. Our names are the first part of ourselves that we share with others. Just the act of acknowledging a name makes a person feel important and accepted. "Words have meaning and names have power"—author unknown. Sharing names shifts people from the role of *strangers* to *acquaintances*, and, eventually, many will transition to *friends* (Roessing 2006, 22). But right now, the first step is to learn the names and maybe a few beginning facts.

GETTING TO KNOW NAMES AND INTERESTS

Students enter the room the first day of class. The teacher's computer is playing the theme from *Cheers*, "Where Everybody Knows Your Name" (Portnoy 2003). Everyone who has ever seen *Cheers* realizes this song is about more than everyone knowing "your name"; it is about everyone knowing *you*. When Norm enters the bar and everyone shouts out, "Norm," they are greeting the man, not the name.

The teacher can project the words to the song and invite students to sing along. Some do, some don't, and already the teacher will have learned something about them.

The song can lead students to journaling about the power of names and people knowing our names, and they can be invited to share. Usually everyone discovers that most adolescents like their names to be known. And then the names can be shared. It is vital to place the seats in a circle so that everyone can see each other and match the name with a face.

There are many variations to name sharing. In one scenario, a student says her name, and the next says his name and the name of the prior student. As they travel around the circle, it obviously gets more challenging, but students are allowed to prompt each other, either with hints from the subject or encouragement from the other students. Already the class is becoming a team. Teachers can also ask students to write their names in marker on a piece of cardstock and, when a student is stumped, hold it up. It helps to associate the person with the name and reinforces memory. This is not a contest or a quiz; help helps.

In another activity, each person says his or her first name and something that she or he likes that starts with the same letter or rhymes with the name. The one disadvantage is that, while alliteration and especially rhyme helps in learning and remembering the names, students tend to choose anything that starts with the letter or rhymes, and, therefore, we do not usually learn anything significant about the students.

"Lesley likes lollypops." [And nothing rhymes with Lesley.]

"Do you really?"

"Not really."

However, with a little more thought and some brainstorming—maybe some categories listed on the board—"Lesley likes literature" would be appropriate for their language arts teacher.

To become familiar with students as more than names and for them to become acquainted with each other, a beginning activity can be to make name signs for their desks. The students print their names, forming each letter into an item that tells something about themselves.

An *L* might be a pencil and a fountain pen. Melissa's *M* was two mountains with her vacation home perched in the valley; one of her *S*'s was a bowl of spaghetti with a strand of pasta *S*-ing from the bowl to the fork. Rachel's *R* was an upside-down curling iron with a cord forming the right side of the R; Dan's *N* consisted of a collection of sports paraphernalia–a hockey stick, a golf club, and a lacrosse stick.

Figure 1.1.   **Kate shares her name and interests.**

Before drawing, students brainstorm a list of favorites—foods, interests, activities, sports, hobbies, places, games, people, school subjects, et cetera. The next step is to match these with letters; designers can use capitals, small letters, or a combination of both. The teacher can advise students to write the name by which they want to be called.

During the time students are designing and creating their signs, classmates chat with their neighbors, sharing supplies and ideas, playing with their names and each other's names, and communicating. When completed, the teacher can ask students to look at each other's signs and tell what they have learned about each other.

"Caitlin has a cat, likes pizza, takes gymnastics, and plays the drums. Hey, Caitlin, are you in band? So am I." Jana has noted a similarity and someone with whom to walk to band class. Her classmates also have learned that she does not like to be called "Cait."

Classmates learn that Mary Kate goes by both names and Dave is all about soccer. Anthony, though small, plays football. Emily has visited London—her *L* is Big Ben. Amber wears black makeup and nail polish but is a ballet dancer, and tiny Jen is earning her black belt in karate. The name signs are also helping to break down stereotypes and value the diversity of the classroom.

While students are connecting through discovered similarities, they are also noticing the diverse talents of their classmates. Caitlin can draw very well, Sarah has a creative sense of color and design, Benjamin meticulously measures out his letters so that he doesn't run out of room on his 8.5-inch-sign, and Tom thinks outside the box.

These facts, such as artistic prowess, are mentally noted by the teacher *and* by their classmates and will be important to know when choosing group members for future projects. It is also easy to observe affective traits—which students are sociable and jabber with everyone, who would rather work alone, who is interested in everyone else's creation, who stays on task, and who are the organizers. ("Let's place sets of markers so that everyone can reach them and each group of four can share a ruler," directs Pat.)

The signs will remain on the desks until they all learn each other's names and become better acquainted; then they are stored in the classroom and brought out periodically for class visitors and speakers, for substitute teachers, and when new students join the class.

This is an activity that can be employed in homeroom or a class. If middle school teachers are employing this activity in multiple classes, they may want to have the students use different topics for each sign. On the other hand, students on the team can carry the sign from class to class, later storing the signs in their homerooms for use with substitute teachers.

During this name sign activity, teachers can play a song about getting to know each other, such as "Getting to Know You" from *The King and I* (Rodgers and Hammerstein 2000). Played softly in the background, it exerts a subliminal message—at least until they all begin humming along.

Teachers whose students do not hum along to songs like "Where Everybody Knows Your Name " and "Getting to Know You" because they are too "dated" can choose more current selections, such as Jim Croce's "I Got a Name," or ask their students to find and share appropriate music with the same theme.

ACTIVITIES TO INTRODUCE OURSELVES

An activity teachers may employ the next day is the Jolly Rancher Activity. Teachers may be tempted to ask students to tell what they want their class to know about them, but the shy or apprehensive student might say nothing and feel threatened. Early adolescence is a difficult time to open up. A goal is also for students to notice similarities between themselves and other students, so it is beneficial to narrow the possible categories that they will use to share something about themselves.

Teachers can pass around a bowl of Jolly Ranchers, Dum Dums, or any other individually wrapped candy that comes in five or six colors and ask students to each chose a candy but not to eat it—yet. It is best to include approximately the same number of candies in each color. If administrators do not allow candy in the classrooms, teachers can distribute playing cards; instead of colors, numbers or suits determine the category the student uses to share. After the students make their choices, the teachers can project a list on the overhead (or uncover it on the board):

Jolly Rancher Activity

RED: best costume or outfit worn/owned

BLUE: favorite present received or given

PURPLE: favorite movie, television show, or book or type of movie, television show, or book

GREEN: favorite type of food

PINK: favorite sport or activity to play or watch

Obviously, these categories can vary. However, it is important that they not be intimidating or too personal; they should be general enough that everyone can answer comfortably but limited enough so that students can find others who share the same interests or preferences. Because some students may not celebrate Halloween, it may be necessary to explain that a "costume" can refer to a dance recital or play as well as to Halloween.

There may be students who cannot afford costumes or are not able to take part in "typical" childhood activities due to a variety of circumstances; therefore, the "outfit" is incorporated. "Watching" should be included in the sports/activities category, as not everyone can play, nor does everyone want to, but many like to watch sports on television or attend sporting events, if only for the snacks. "Activities" eliminates arguments over whether cheerleading or sailing is a sport.

Teachers are always amazed at how much they learn about students through these categories, especially "best present." The students themselves are more interested in who likes what movie or television show, as this category sparks the most conversation among them. Again, they are focusing on similarities and are interested in the differences. ("What's bocce?")

An alternate activity can be employed in an additional team class so that students are building relationships in all classes but not repeating activities. This type of activity is referred to as the Paired-Squared activity, although it seldom works out to mathematically fit the title. Students sit in pairs and find five or six things they have in common (besides being in the same grade, being the same age, going to the same middle school, and having the same teacher). They then join with another pair and find four things they *all* have in common. Each quad joins with another, and they find three things all eight share.

The class then comes together and finds two things from their lists that everyone has in common. If there is nothing, they all brainstorm together. Even if they finally finish with only "we are in the same grade, same school, same academic team, and same class," they have acknowledged membership in a common group. Unless they have classes of multiples of eight, teachers will need to play with the numbers, possibly breaking up groups to join with other groups; teachers with class sizes of thirty-two can include one more round.

A modification is for each student to walk around with a list of classmates' names and find one different thing in common with each classmate. As classmates learn about each other and realize that they have *something* in common with *everyone*, they also notice that everyone is a bit different, even members of their group.

"I AM" AND "WE ARE" POETRY

One final introductory activity introduces the class as both a cohort of individuals and a cohesive group working together throughout the year. This is the class "I Am" poem. The typical format for this poetry follows, but verbs can be altered either by the teacher or by the individual students to fit their lives more closely.

☙

I am . . . an eighth grade student.°
I wonder . . .
I hear . . .
I see . . .
I want . . .
I am . . .

I pretend . . .
I feel . . .
I touch . . .
I worry . . .
I cry . . .
I am . . .
I understand . . .
I say . . .
I dream . . .
I try . . .
I hope . . .
I am [name of student].

°Added to the standard "I am" poem format. Teachers can be specific with the name of the school, team, or class.

Teachers then demonstrate with an example from an anonymous student:

I am a new eighth grade student.
I wonder how my classes will go this year, how hard the work will be.
I hear my teacher telling us her plans for the year; I listen and I don't
    understand.
I see my classmates; many seem to already know each other.
I want to fit in with them.
I am a little nervous about classes, sports, and making friends.

I pretend I am in seventh grade again, safe with what I already know.
I feel the air crackle with newness and a kind of excitement.
I touch my textbook and wonder if I am up to the challenge.
I worry that I will not be able to fit everything in: homework, dancing,
    sports . . .
I cry for the victims in our social studies units: early settlers with dy-
    ing children and
the Native Americans who were displaced (this year the Civil War
    widows);
I am much too emotional for my own good.

I understand that this year will decide what classes I can take in high school.
I say, "I think I can; I think I can," like the Little Engine That Could.
I dream of going away to a big university, maybe Duke.
I try to take life one step at a time.
I hope I make friends, get A's, and have fun.
I am Sarah, now an eighth grader.

As the students create their poems, teachers should assure them that they will not have to share their poem with the class. However, when they are finished, they are requested to mark a star or an asterisk next to one line—other than the first or last—that they are willing to share. Before sharing, they revise the line to make it, as Samuel Taylor Coleridge said, "the best words in the best order" and expand it as much as they can.

Everyone stands in a circle and each reads his or her highlighted line as they go around the room. Each student can read his name and his line, or they each read the starred line and the class then circles the room one more time, reading the last lines, their names. The teacher can end the recitation by adding, "We are the _____ grade students of [class, team, school]."

Without actually pointing it out, the class can detect how much richer the poem is when most students have something different to say; however, it is also clear that areas of repetition are also effective. Their different voices and melodies have become an orchestral composition.

The students can then type their poems and, during the school year, whenever individuals feel comfortable, display them on one of the class bulletin boards.

This activity was employed with a fifth grade humanities class at a South Carolina private school. The "I am" format was introduced; the teacher modeled her "I Am" poem so that they could see the format. How to expand the lines to give even more information was illustrated, and students drafted their poems. When they had had some time to revise, they were asked to put a star next to the line either that they liked the best or that contained information they wanted to share with their peers.

Their poem showed a diversity of interests and ideas:

I am Alex; I can succeed in sports and in life.
I am Shalina; I smell perfection when I try the best that I can.
I am Sari; I wonder about the future . . . What will happen. My job.
   My life . . .
I am Emily; I understand how Nicole [fellow student] feels about
   leaving her friends in Pennsylvania.
I am Nicole; I am a mystery awaiting to be seeked [sic].
I am Jackson; I cry never because I am tough.
I am Alyssa; I see the butterflies that swarm around the flowers.
I am Noah; I miss my Uncle Matt because he's an air force pilot and
   is stationed in Japan.
I am Davis; I say, "Go big or go home."
I am Abigail; I see the beautiful rainbow lights on Dove Street with
   hot chocolate in my hands.
I am Sam; I hear the roaring sound that blasts from my amp.
I am Kylie; I say those who say happiness only comes with sunshine
   have never danced in the rain.
I am Kelsey; I see her [my grandmother] in the clouds when I'm
   thinking about her having a wonderful time with my grandpa.
I am Mrs. B-C, your teacher; I dream of a world where men seek
   peace through sharing words, not violence and reaction.
WE ARE the 5-A humanities class.

When asked to write a reflection on what they learned during the activity, Emily wrote, "I learned that people are all alike in different ways."
This was the "takeaway" teachers can hope for.

Eighth grade students in a public school across town with vastly different demographics engaged in the same activity. Since it was a little
later in the school term, many of the students nodded as their classmates read, their lines supporting what they already knew about each
other; others learned even more about their peers that day.

I am a student in Ms. Martin's first period class.
I dream of a better tomorrow where there is no violence and people
   can just get along for the sake of our lives.

I wonder why people have to destroy nature.

I say I don't care, but I die inside.

I dream of a day when the clouds will sing in harmony.

I am shy, but loud at times—at least when I need to be.

I want to be a better person each day, changing my attitude and perspective.

I am a mystery, hiding who I am, now and then letting myself bloom. Only for an instant so you see the real me.

I am flawed but dynamic; I am fearful but courageous.

I hear the inside of me screaming to be heard by the outside world. I am someone;

I am a good friend. Talk to me; I am listening.

I wonder about what will happen in my future.

I want to go many more places in my life to meet different people.

I pretend that I am Leonardo da Vinci when he draws the Mona Lisa, painting the luscious lips and diamond eyes.

I sing a song that no one else will ever hear.

I am the definition of a strong, beautiful, smart African-American woman, still standing, heading into the game.

We are a class of eighth grade students of Ridgeland Middle School.

By this time and through these types of activities, the teacher and students know each other's names and also a little bit about each other. The activities have primarily focused on similarities, but everyone has noted some of the differences, and, hopefully, students will begin to see these as strengths. The class is on our way to becoming an *us*.

2

STARTING WITH SIMILARITIES

In Mem Fox's picture book *Feathers and Fools* (1996), two groups of birds, the peacocks and the swans, become focused on their differences. This focus turns into apprehension of the *other*. The peacocks' observation of what *could* happen leads to suspicion and fear, which, in turn, transforms into distrust by the swans. Panic leads to war in which all the birds are slaughtered.

However, in the time that follows, two eggs hatch, one a baby peacock and the other a swan. Trusting innocents, they run to each other and focus on their similarities. They notice that they both have feathers, two legs, a head, and two eyes and decide that they shall be friends.

"So off they went together, in peace and unafraid, to face the day and share the world."

Small children do just that—they accept each other because they realize they are all small children and don't generally look beyond that similarity. Gordon Allport (1979) explained in *The Nature of Prejudice* how all young children will play together until prejudices are learned and acquired. Unfortunately, prejudice can start at an early age. Working with adolescents, many times teachers have to overcome prejudice and distrust of an out-group.

As a first step, teachers can guide adolescents to focus on their similarities, creating the view that they and their classmates are a "tribe," that together they compose one peer group. "As children become adolescents, they become more independent, and yet they have 'precarious identities'; consequently they seek new identities and personal security from peer groups" (Allport 1976).

A number of activities and discussions can take place during homeroom times or advisement periods to stress the sense of homeroom as a "home base." Many adolescents acquire that sense of belonging from joining sports teams, but not everyone belongs to a team, and at times even team members are placed in situations of competing with each other for positions and playing time, accentuating their differences. Students are not necessarily in classes with all of their peers from homeroom, and, therefore, homeroom can become a safe haven, a place where they are noncompeting "family" members.

At times, students in homerooms do not even know each other's names at the end of the year, because there is none of the interaction that takes place in a classroom. Homeroom teachers can let students become acquainted during this time spent together. Discovering students with similar interests by categories such as movies, music, hobbies, sports, or video games and then holding discussion group times where different groups can discuss their favorites together is a luxury for which content area classes do not have time.

The students can generate topics and divide themselves by interests. An interest discussion day can be held once a week or month, and the homeroom teacher or the students themselves can bring in articles to read and discuss, generating more informational text reading. One teacher had in her homeroom three students who raised ferrets; one even showed hers. They had quite a lot in common, and not many others were interested in discussing ferret topics in depth.

A weekly or biweekly game day allows the checker players, the chess players, the card players, and the board game players to interact and bond. Teachers may often see students who never hang out together at other times and are not in the same classes form chess friendships. One homeroom had a calligraphy group while another gathering was crafting bracelets out of some type of thread. The members of those groups enjoyed the fact that they could sit together and share techniques and materials while listening to the morning announcements.

Homeroom periods can be brief, filled with other activities, such as role-taking and announcements and students coming in and out from other activities, and not all schools have activity or club periods. Therefore, affective activities should also take place within the curricula of classes. Time is short, and standards rule the classroom, so activities that focus on the similarities of students necessitate a fit with the curriculum.

ENGLISH/LANGUAGE ARTS CLASS

Playing word games in language arts classes serves a double function: students increase their vocabularies and word sense, and affective time is provided for classmates to connect. There are many word games, such as Scrabble, which allow students to find others who share their interests and talents, whether it is through the type of word games they like (crossword puzzles, Scrabble, Taboo, or the artistic Pictionary) or through what they find out about each other as they play the games. Either way, word games further their vocabulary skills and also fulfill language arts standards.

As illustrated in chapter 1, poetry is an effective way for students to "academically" share their stories. Beside "I Am" poetry, poetry in "Two Voices" can be successful and allow for instruction in writing elements, poetic devices, and performance techniques. Students can learn much about each other when they write two-voice poetry. Poems for two voices compare and contrast two things, people, or in the case of Paul Fleischman's (1988) *Joyful Noise: Poems for Two Voices*, the lives of insects. In "Honeybees," Fleischman compares the life of the queen bee to that of a worker bee. The queen bee explains why, to her, "Being a bee is a joy," while, at the same time, the worker complains, "Being a bee is a pain" (29–31). While these two do not find many similarities in their lives, teachers can use this poem as an example of poems in two voices, a format used to focus on similarities.

An example of the process is illustrated in the poem "Teenagers" (Roessing 2005, 8), although the poet compares herself to a person she has never actually met (figure 2.1). Reading Esmeralda Santiago's memoir *When I Was Puerto Rican* and contemplating the two-voice poetry format, the poet wondered, "What could I possibly have in common

TEENAGERS (in response to *When I Was Puerto Rican* by Esmerralda Santiago)
by Lesley Roessing

Being a teenager was hard in the Sixties.	Being a teenager was hard in the Sixties.
I was a European-American	I was
girl.	a Puerto-Rican girl.
I grew up in western Pennsylvania.	I grew up in
in a small town.	Puerto Rico in a small village.
We never moved	We moved back and forth many times; We finally came to New York
We were the *hicks*.	We were *jibaro*.
Same thing. But my father made a very good living;	Same thing.
Although he was an artist.	*My* father could barely support us; Although he was a poet.
In school I never felt the same as everybody else.	In school I never felt the same as everybody else. "Spic"
"Jew."	
But in high school I did well. Academics were important to me.	But in high school I did well. Academics were important to me.
I liked attention and to perform	I liked attention and to perform
which caused me to become a teacher.	which caused me to become
	a writer.
We are both storytellers, telling the stories of ourselves and others.	We are both storytellers, telling the stories of ourselves and others.

Figure 2.1.

with a sixteen-year-old Puerto Rican girl who grew up in the Caribbean and, in her early teens, moved to New York City?" Frantically she searched her family tree for a lone Latino relative among the Russian-Polish immigrants on both sides. She tried to ignore her middle-class rural western Pennsylvanian roots and searched through Santiago's memoir, focusing on the diverse culture of its subject, thinking of it as a book about "them," not "us."

Desperate to discover any similarities, the poet started turning pages more slowly and noticed dates in the text. With a shock, she realized that she and Santiago were sixteen years old the same year! After discovering that one commonality, it was not difficult to find another, and another. They had both faced prejudices in their communities—the small town, the new land. They both liked center stage—one as an actress, the other a teacher. They both are writers. They were practically twins! The poem grew and grew, illustrating that when we look for similarities, we find them.

Poetry in two voices is written in two columns; the phrases that are the same are lined up across from each other. This type of poem is meant to be read aloud by two people. It is an aural experience and can be very powerful when the two voices enter in unison, stressing the similarities. Read silently, it can also become a visual experience.

Teachers can use this format extensively to assist students in finding similarities with people of other times and cultures, but it can also be employed for students to discover similarities with other classmates, becoming *us*, rather than "us" and "them."

Students can pair randomly or choose a partner they do not know well, and together they brainstorm areas of similarities. John might like basketball and Tom baseball, but they both like to participate in team sports (figure 2.2).

Together the class brainstorms areas in which to pursue similarities, topics which may not occur to many students as they search for likenesses. John and Thomas continue their collaborative, coauthored poem (figure 2.3).

Sometimes very surprising similarities surface, and these particularly serve as a bonding experience.

A fifth grade teacher implemented this activity in her language arts class and shared a poem written by two of her students (figure 2.4).

JOHN	THOMAS
I like to play team sports.	I like to play team sports.
Basketball.	
	Baseball is my favorite.
I play for my school.	I play for my school
	And community.

Figure 2.2.

JOHN	**THOMAS**
I like to play team sports;	I like to play team sports;
Basketball.	
	Baseball.
I play for my school	I play for my school
	and community.
We take annual summer trips to	We take annual summer trips to
the Mountains;	
	the Seashore;
I miss my friends but make new ones.	I miss my friends but make new ones.
Stuck with a little brother,	Stuck with an older brother,
Vacations are sometimes a pain!	Vacations are sometimes a pain!
When we celebrate Christmas,	
	When we celebrate Hanukah,
We wrap our presents in different	We wrap our presents in different
paper for each family member.*	paper for each family member.*
We have a dinner with neighbors	We have a dinner with family
	on the first night.
on Christmas Eve.	
My family watches television together	My family watches television together
every night.	
	Sometimes.
My favorite television shows are	My favorite television shows are
about crime and forensics—	about crime and forensics—
Cold Case.	
	NCIS-LA.
We both have a busy, teenage life.	We both have a busy, teenage life.

Figure 2.3.

Similarities Topics

Family members
Sports, activities, hobbies, games, clubs
Foods, types of food
Ethnicities, nationalities, neighborhoods, elementary schools
Favorite school subjects, academic strengths
Talents, interests, goals, dreams
Vacations, holidays, customs
Movies, books, television shows—specific or by genre
Any favorites

Their teacher found that even though the point of the lesson—finding similarities—was never stated, this was the one "takeaway" from the poetry exercise. After writing and performing these two-voice poems, students were asked to write "something they learned and something that they liked in the assignment." Kwame wrote, "I learned that there is another way to do poetry. I like that me and my partner have a lot in common."

Correspondingly, his partner, Hayden, wrote down, "I learned that Kwame and I have a lot in common." Another student in the class, Quinn, noted, "I learned about the person [with whom she wrote her poem]. I liked the activity," while Kacy wrote, "I liked finding similarities about Elle and I."

This poetry activity compels students to work collaboratively toward a common goal while serving to highlight their similarities, and it also fosters connections between students. The assignment also serves as lessons in writing, poetry, compare-contrast text structure, and public speaking (choral reading), all components of a conventional language arts curriculum and certain to match state standards.

BEING US

Kwame   *Hayden*

We've been friends for six years

We've even been in the same class

except for last year...

I was in Mrs. N's class.

I was in Mrs. D's.

We love sports!

Football, I've played for four years.

I've played hockey for five.

We love cool, cool colors.

Blue.

Purple—it's the color of my room.

We both celebrate

Christmas-time holidays...

I celebrate Christmas   I celebrate Christmas.

and Kwanza.

And we like ice cream:

Cookies and Cream.

Chocolate Chip Cookie Dough.

Being me...

Kwame.   Hayden.

Figure 2.4.

MATHEMATICS CLASS

In mathematics classes, students can also work within their prescribed curriculum while discovering, and charting, commonalities with their classmates. This math class activity focuses on students' parallel interests and could supplement a lesson, or unit, on charts and graphs.

Students make a list of different favorites categories or "faves":

- Ice cream flavors
- Types of music
- Types of movies
- Pizza toppings
- Holidays
- School subjects
- Highlighter color

The class divides into groups of four—one group for each topic—and each group polls the class for their particular topic. Collaboratively, each group makes a graph of the results, depending on what they have learned about graphs in class. Graphs work well because they communicate information visually; students can decide as a group what type of graph would be most effective, the teacher can assign a different graph type to each group, or one type of graph can be assigned and results in different categories can be compared and contrasted.

The graphs are then posted around the room for students to view and even compare to other math classes. Later the graphs can be revised into other formats studied in upcoming math classes (bar graphs to circle graphs, statistical analyses, etc.), and students can discuss which type of representation is more appropriate or effective. This activity can also be employed to study percentages.

It is important to note that even if only one student is represented in a particular category, such as spinach as a favorite pizza topping, he is nevertheless part of the record as a percentage of the class and, therefore, a part of *us* (figures 2.5, 2.6).

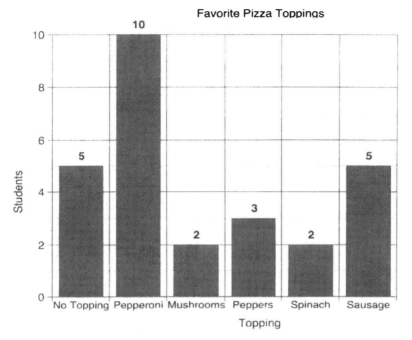

Figure 2.5.

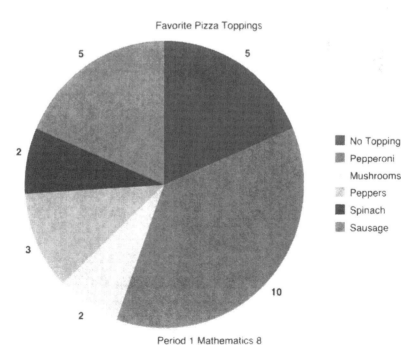

Figure 2.6.

SOCIAL STUDIES CLASS

The social sciences include various fields that concern past and current human behavior and interactions. The National Council for the Social Studies (2012) defines the discipline as "the integrated study of the social sciences and humanities to promote civic competence." The organization believes that effective social studies programs include experiences that provide for the study of, among others, culture; time, continuity, and change; people, places, and environment; and individual development and identity.

Even though the social studies curricula of different schools vary, and students study diverse locations and historic times, focusing on the "social studies" aspects of these courses takes us back to the fact that people are products of the effects of environment. Many times adolescents can find connections when they focus on where they came from and what made them who they are.

Examining our origins tends to strip away some differences, bringing out similarities, and also serves to introduce adolescents to the backgrounds of their peers. In these remembrances, adolescents do not focus on differences in socioeconomic status—after all, playing hopscotch on a venue scratched out with a stone is the same as playing on a court made with large pieces of expensive colored chalk—or many of the other cultural disparities that really do not matter.

Cynthia Rylant's autobiographical picture book *When I Was Young in the Mountains* (1982) tells the story of using the "johnny house" in the middle of the night without commenting on the lack of indoor facilities. And nobody would censure her for a lifestyle that many would consider lacking in monetary assets; life was what it was, and the book shares the author's fond memories.

Everyone has heard the stories of the humble beginnings of many of our "stars" and money moguls, such as Oprah Winfrey. Just experiencing childhood is a critical equalizer.

In her poem "Where I'm From," George Ella Lyon (1999) shares her childhood, her home, and her relatives. She begins with the sights and smells of the laundry on the line (clothespins and Clorox) and her father's dry-cleaning business (carbon tetrachloride). Many of us remember the scents of childhood—clothes drying on the line—and have climbed a favorite tree until we have memorized each branch, those that held our weight and those that did not.

Ms. Lyon goes on to share family sayings ("perk up") and family stories, both of which we all have too many. Relatives, religion, and foods show the readers of her poem from where and whom and what she came.

One teacher modeled with her own "Where I'm From" poem, appropriately named "Back in the 'Hood," ("'Hood" referring to both the neighborhood and childhood).

Back in the 'Hood
by Lesley Roessing (with thanks to George Ella Lyon)

I am from King-of-the-Mountain,
Hide-and-Seek, Statues, and Tag.
Splashing in puddles on rainy days and
Cowboys and Indians, Cops 'n' Robbers.

I am from maples trees and weeping willows,
Rose bushes, Tiger Lilies, and Forsythia,
Playing in portable pools on sunny days and
Pennies in the patio cement, one for each child.

I am from the Beegleys and the Painters,
The Krols, the Wards, and the Weges,
Visiting neighbors' porches and kitchens and
Walkways and steps, even those that didn't house children.

I am from paper dolls and Mr. Machine,
Hula Hoops, Betsy Wetsy, and Barbies,
Playing hopscotch on driveways and jacks on linoleum floors, and
Penny candy that actually cost a penny.

I am from ballet lessons and piano lessons,
Brownies, 4-H Club, and the Country Club,
Building cabins among the May apples and Jack-in-the-Pulpits and
Shana, trotting behind me on all my quests.

I am from Ozzie and Harriet and Donna Reed,
Lassie, The Lone Ranger, and I Love Lucy,
Watching movies at the Route 19 Drive-in and
Strawberry pie from Big Boy.

I am from a small town and tree-filled yards,
Family dinners, barbecuing, and birthday parties,
Storing memories to build big dreams—
Endless with possibilities.

Even though the students could not identify with watching *Ozzie and Harriet*, many have seen *I Love Lucy*. They haven't eaten at Big Boy as had their teacher who grew up in western Pennsylvania, but they have grown up with its contemporary or geographic equivalents. Today's students' version of King-of-the-Mountain is Capture the Flag, and even most immigrant students have played a version of Hide-and-Seek. Hopscotch is played all over the world. Barbie is still around, although Mr. Machine has bitten the dust of greater technology.

After reading "Where I'm From," students wrote their own shadow poems. Doug shared his childhood fears and triumphs stemming from a vivid imagination:

I'm from the jungle
Where I found my first salamander.
I scratched my knee,
And the scar leaves tracks—
Digs in my mind,
And refuses to leave.
I'm from the jungle.

I'm from the fort
Where I hid from enemies,
Hid from the monsters.
Names scream off the walls
And tickle my ears,
Carves names in the mind.
I'm from the fort.

I'm from the cave
Where I play hide-and-go-seek.
Lines of clothes were my disguise,
"Stealth" they call me,
For I can't be seen by the naked eye,
Hiding routes in the web of my mind.
I'm from the cave.

I'm from the battlefield
Where I searched for the enemies,
That I must capture.
But when it's my turn to run,
So much like lightning,
It burns my mind.
I'm from the battlefield.

I'm from the imagination.
Time has passed,
But memories remain,
For the imagination lingered
And struck my weary mind.
I remember most, but not all.
I'm from imagination.

Janel's story was a different one:

I am from barbecue,
From corn-on-the-cob and mac-and-cheese.
I am from mowed grass and tall trees.
I am from the never-finished playground
That has no swing or benches
As if time stood still before my eyes.

I am from teachers and scientists,
From Mandela and Martin Luther King.
I'm from "Don't do drugs"
And "Stay in school."
From *Respect* and *Be tactful*.
I'm from "Thank you, Jesus"
From children's church
And the gospel songs
I've heard many times before.

I'm from word games and puzzles,
Road trips and airplane rides.
But also from drive-by shootings
And trying to stay alive.

In my room are boxes
Toppling over with old pictures—

A time when I lived
With no care at all,
A time that I will never forget
And never want to erase.

Sharing and comparing, students found that they all played hide-and-go-seek and tag or its equivalent in another country. They all had forts, even if they were made of sheets or blankets. All mothers or parental figures have the same platitudes in any language: "I don't care what your friends do. If they all jumped off a cliff [bridge], would you follow them?" and "If you keep making that face, it will freeze that way." Having to go to Sunday (or Saturday) school is pretty much the same, no matter the religion.

Because they grew up during the same time period, many adolescents played with the same toys. The day P.J. brought in his Fisher-Price pirate ship for a memoir show-and-tell in language arts class, choruses of "I had one of those!" filled the room. He instantly was surrounded by a group of boys, sharing pirate ship stories and games.

The "Where I'm From" poems won't be the same. Everyone's past is at least a little different, and poets may focus on different memories, but the sentiments are the same. Adolescents can sympathize with each other's growing pains, and somehow they don't evaluate each other's past as they do the present. The most important aspect of the assignment is that students learn about each other and possibly why they are who they are.

An alternate assignment would be to model on Cynthia Rylant's book *When I Was Young in the Mountains* with a shadow picture book or poem, "When I Was Young in _____.

This type of assignment is generally too personal with which to begin the year, but it can be utilized to lead into a curriculum-based research assignment in which students choose a historical figure they are studying, research his or her past, and turn the research into a "Where I'm From" poem, analyzing the person's later decisions and motivations. Ulysses S. Grant and Robert E. Lee most likely had disparate childhoods but possibly many similar components. "I don't care what your friends do, Ulysses [Robert]. If they all jumped off a cliff, would you follow them?"

Rather than poetry or picture books, students can generate their writings from country music models, such as Kenny Chesney's "Back Where I Come From" (McAnally 1996), Alan Jackson's (2007) "Where I Come From," or Sugarland's (2004a) "Hello" or (2004b) "Small Town Jericho."

This again brings music into the classroom, and there are plenty more origination stories within the country music venue. Students may suggest songs from other musical genres that they can imitate.

SCIENCE CLASS

Science generally does not lend itself to the personal; but taking science fiction one step closer, what if students were to write "If I Were" poems or prose? Metaphors are effective communication tools because, through them, we compare the unknown to the known, i.e., "Sarah is a walking dictionary."

During the study of chemistry, labeling themselves as a elements and then comparing themselves with other students, adolescents can appreciate how their classmates perceive themselves: "I am iron, hard but lustrous and vital to life," or "I see myself as hydrogen, light but the most abundant element in the atmosphere." Beryllium with a high melting point defines the teen who is slow to anger; titanium is the opposite, being "marvelous in fireworks."

Pairing students to combine "their" elements into compounds would be an interesting way to combine personalities and would determine how they could effectively work together, turning their differences (hydrogen and oxygen) into a similarity (water).

Within the study of the universe, students could each choose the planet they are most like: Mars—red (hair or temperament), the god of war; Venus—bright, also representing love and beauty; Jupiter—large, the king of the gods, the planet has stormy "temperament" but also the most moons (followers); Neptune represents one who loves the sea; Pluto—small, cast off and demoted to a dwarf planet; Uranus always causes embarrassment; and the Sun—need we say more about this child? Men may be from Mars, but so is Ellen.

FOREIGN LANGUAGE CLASS

In many middle grades foreign language classes, students choose names from the cultures they are studying. What a perfect time this would be to study their own names and the cultures from which *they* come! Through names, adolescents can discover obscure similarities to other students and initiate an interest in their diversity.

Students can investigate the origination of their first, or given, names and explore the meanings of their own names in different languages. Many students discover that their names are of very different ethnic origins than they are. The name "Bridget" is Irish, and Bridget may very well be part Irish, but Colleen's family heritage is Italian-German.

In one primarily Christian school district, Rebecca, Rachel, and Joe are all surprised, as are many others, that the origin of their names is Hebrew, until they remember that those names appear in the Old Testament. Jesse is not aware that his name is in the Old Testament, but instantly he has a connection to Rachel, Rebecca, and Joseph, and now Leah who actually is Jewish.

Some students are linked by the meanings of their names. Abrafo (African), Andre and Louis (French), Earl (Old English), Andrew (Greek), Kimble (Welsh), Quan (Vietnamese), Shaheed (Islamic), Takeo (Japanese), and Wyatt (English) are all names signifying a form of "warrior." The meanings and ethnic origins of their names are just one way students can see similarities between themselves and others whom they might have seen as "different."

Teachers can also facilitate students in identifying parallels through their names by illustrating the ways in which names have been transformed in divergent languages and cultures. In America one of the more common male given names is "John," originally a Hebrew name. The variant "Sean" exists in Ireland; however, "Sean" has also become a common given name in America, making the top 100 male names in the 1990s and becoming even more popular in the 2000s.

And that directs the class to the female derivatives, such as Joan and Joanne, and their variants in different cultures. All of a sudden, uncommon names cease to be so "weird," and students, such as Mary and Maria, Michael and Michelle, find others who share their names. While "Ivan" might seem strange to an American teen, the fact that it is a form of "John" may eliminate the fear of the unknown, sometimes the basis of xenophobia.

Variants of John

Sean—Irish	Jan—Dutch, Polish
Jon/Jonathan—British	Janek—Polish, Czech
Shawn—English	Hans—Danish
Evan—Welsh	Jon—Scandinavian
Ian—Scottish	Johann—German
Jean—French	Giovanni—Italian
Ivan—Russian	Ioannis—Greek
Juan—Spanish	Yahya—Arabic, Turkish

The study of the ways in which family names, or surnames, originated also guides students to make connections with their classmates. In many cultures, there were originally four common types of surname: patronymics, place names, professions, and descriptive names.

Patronymics were last names derived from the first name of the son's father plus "son." William, son of John, became William Johnson. Robert, son of William, became Robert Williamson, later in some cases shortened to Williams and even Wilson. Students can look at their names and determine who might have a name that was originally a patronymic. But here again, they need to study the cultural variants.

-son: English and American	-opoulos: Greek
-sohn: German	-ian/-yan: Armenian
-sen: Danish, Norwegian	Mc-, Mac-: Irish, Scottish
-zoon: Dutch	O': Irish, Scottish (grandson of)
-ez: Spanish	Fitz-: Norman
-es: Portuguese	Ap-: Welsh
-ovich: Russian	-bin-: Arabic
-ovych: Ukrainian	-ben-: Hebrew
-ovic: Serbian	

John Johnson and Ivan Ivanovich, two names that sound very different, are really name twins.

Some cultures also employ matronymics, such as "-dottir" in Iceland; but even though a few cultures, such as Pakistan, still use the patronymic system, surnames have become static, and, therefore, also female students can compare their names.

Other means for forming surnames were place names ("Rivers"), professions ("Smith"), and descriptive names ("Short"). Working with their foreign language teachers, students can ascertain what their surnames might be in translation—as *Schwartz,* German for "black"—even allowing for changes through the decades and through immigration practices. This is a fun and purposeful way to study language and cultures, and to uncover yet another similarity to classmates.

MUSIC CLASS

In music class, students can imitate the math activity, minus the graph construction, and group themselves by favorite music genres, artists, composers, and/or songs. Each group can then plan a lesson in which they teach their preference to the rest of the class, thereby allowing some classmates to discover a new style. For example, the group who has a partiality to country music could research and introduce country songs and share their predilection with the rappers who, in turn, would do the same.

At another point in the term, students with similar interests can work together, writing a song that follows the model of their favorite genre or artist. Musical groups can also find ways to connect their favorite genres or musicians, building a bridge between the music and, thereby, the other adolescent groups. For instance, aspiring musicians could explore what one type of music has in common with another or create a musical with each song as represented by a different style of music—a pluralistic musical.

Throughout the first months of the year, all classes can incorporate a few experiences that allow students to discover their similarities and, therefore, work together that much more effectively and collaboratively.

③

BECOMING PART OF THE PUZZLE

After students connect through a recognition of similarities and become comfortable with each other, the opportunity arrives to teach adolescents the value of diversity, especially the diversity among their peers. There are many obvious similarities, being that they are all adolescents, and they have identified more similarities through the activities in chapters 1 and 2. Once adolescents have established connections, the next step is demonstrating to students the power of diversity.

As American writer and social activist Robert Alan is attributed with saying, "Cultural differences should not separate us from each other, but rather cultural diversity brings a collective strength that can benefit all humanity."

Article 1 of the Universal Declaration on Cultural Diversity (2001) adopted by UNESCO affirms,

> As a source of exchange, innovation and creativity, cultural diversity is as necessary for humankind as biodiversity is for nature. In this sense, it is the common heritage of humanity and should be recognized and affirmed for the benefit of present and future generations.

Many times acknowledging and accepting diversity as strength is outside students' experiences or comfort zones. It is up to the teacher to illustrate to students that their class, their team, their school, and their nation are stronger because of differences, rather than similarities.

Diversity allows us to be greater—more innovative and creative. The whole is greater than the sum of its parts.

An example is our own nation where one basis for our strength is our diversity. In his essay "America: A World of Difference," Oscar Handlin (1986) describes the melting pot theory, and he celebrates the fact that America did *not* become a melting pot where everyone is the same. Instead Handlin proposes the metaphor of an orchestra to describe our nation.

METAPHOR FOR AMERICA—AND *US*

> Some Americans [by 1900] began to question the melting pot idea. They saw no value to uniformity as an end in itself and pointed out that the immigrant and other groups could serve the nation most effectively if they kept their identity and enriched the culture of the whole with their own special contributions. It was like an orchestra, the instruments of which did not play in unison, but joined in a general harmony. (Handlin, 1986, 6)

To explore the idea of diversity as an asset, students can extend the metaphor of America as an orchestra and the people as instruments. One class brainstormed many ways they could divide and classify the components of an orchestra:

- Division 1: the four sections—brass, wind, percussion, and strings
- Division 2: the instruments within each section
- Division 3: the individual musicians who sometimes play solos, sometimes play together in harmony, sometimes play the same notes
- Division 4: the music, the notes, the compositions, the program

There were many directions in which to go; one class chose as examples

- For the sections—wind
- For the instruments within the sections—oboes

- For variants of these instruments from different countries—the Indian shehnai (a North Indian oboe)
- The different oboists in the section

Students then worked their way from general to specific, from the United States as a country to the different types of people:

- Orchestra: America
- Sections: one group of students suggested the geographical areas as they have established their regional identities (the West); another class suggested the races. This might be an effective time to discuss "race" as a social, not biological, construct and encourage the students toward other categorizations, such as immigrants from different continents (Asians). During the ensuing discussion, students realized that they were speaking of "race" as cultural experiences rather than skin color
- Instruments: ethnicities of the people by country (i.e., Japanese); either the settlers in the geographical regions or ethnicities within races
- Musicians: one class suggested the different native languages of our peoples while another class suggested individual talents and exceptionalities; a third class suggested religions

The metaphor extension can become a bit complex since demographics have greatly changed and the United States includes citizens with multiple nationalities, races, and ethnicities, and religions that cross ethnic borders. This complexity adds value to the assignment; it causes the students to stop and analyze. For example, they consider ways in which the individual instruments, which fit nicely into an orchestra section, compare to an individual who might not "fit" into one category.

When students discuss the early development of America, as they are in Handlin's metaphor, the citizens seem not as complex as we now are. A student's great-grandparents may have all been members of one ethnicity and nationality and practiced one religion; but the grandchildren of those great-grandparents may have one nationality and a mixture of many ethnicities and parents who practiced different religions. But they still create an orchestra that is richer for all the different "sounds."

In the same way, there are now musical instruments that cross lines, such as the banjo uke or banjolele, and synthesizers which mimic them all. This is the point of the lesson.

The metaphor of an orchestra raises a variety of discussions. Students find themselves analyzing musical compositions and noting places where instruments from all four sections harmonize, where instruments solely from one section play, and where and when soloists are featured. As instruments and sections are added, the music swells and becomes richer. The most beneficial discussions will be those that lead to the insight the orchestra members have to work together to produce music that is harmonious and rich.

Hubert Humphrey agreed; in one speech as vice president of the United States, Humphrey (1967) compared America to a tapestry:

> Fortunately, the time has long passed when people liked to regard the United States as some kind of melting pot, taking men and women from every part of the world and converting them into standardized, homogenized Americans. We are, I think, much more mature and wise today. Just as we welcome a world of diversity, so we glory in an America of diversity—an America all the richer for the many different and distinctive strands of which it is woven.

As did Maya Angelou (1993): "We all should know that diversity makes for a rich tapestry, and we must understand that all the threads of the tapestry are equal in value no matter their color."

After expanding Handlin's metaphor, the next step is for students to create metaphors for our country and the American people. They always are likely to discover that whatever the metaphor, all illustrate that each person is an indispensable piece of the puzzle (another metaphor). Students have proposed such metaphors as a crayon box, an artist's palette, bouillabaisse, a song, a painting or collage, a pizza, an ocean, or a garden. Some are simple, some more complex.

An innovative metaphor compared America to a book—a collection of paragraphs, sentences, words, and letters, which "cannot do much on [their] own," that also includes characters, plotlines, and settings. Together it can make a masterpiece.

As the next stage, students collaboratively design a metaphor for their class. However, prior to doing so, students need to become better acquainted with their peers to appreciate the diversity the class offers. Then the class collaboratively creates one metaphor, and small groups extend it as they see fit. Individual students are not named.

One class saw themselves as a flower garden. Their garden had five daisies; four marigolds—one yellow, two gold, and one variegated; insects such as bees, moths, and butterflies; some flowering shrubs, and some nonflowering bushes. How did they see themselves in these ways?

Five girls saw themselves as daisies—pretty much alike according to the criteria they were using. It was that criteria that determined the daisy classification: long, thin stems and white petals, but daisies can be different colors, have a fuzzy center, grow in groups (social), and always appear to be "happy" (according to these young ladies).

The "marigolds" liked the idea that even though the flower is not prickly, it wards off deer. They also appreciated the fact that marigolds are similar enough to be identifiable as the same flower, but there are two different sizes and three color varieties, all in the same color family. The variegated marigolds appreciated the idea that they "could be somewhat like the yellows and somewhat like the oranges."

The "insects" saw themselves as a different species than the flowers, and students chose insects that mimicked their personalities.

Students wrote two-line metaphors—the comparison and an explanation—substantiating their choices. Sarah wrote, "I am a butterfly; I flit from idea to idea, never resting more than a few minutes on one before moving to the next." The bee, which can sting, can also make honey and is necessary to make the flowers bloom.

These classmates saw themselves as integral parts of a mutual, symbiotic environment. Everyone fit in and had a place. Certainly the bush might take up more space, but it provided shade from the hot sun for the delicate flowers.

A project such as this makes a picturesque bulletin board, a visual of the class that reminds the class of the strength and beauty in their differences. Picture a garden with flowers, insect life, birds, trees and shrubs, and even a few butterflies, all representing the diversity of culture in the class.

There will also be classes that have to dig deep to find the diversity, illustrating that the classes that teachers sometimes see as more of a challenge *because* of their diversity, such as in socioeconomic status and/or exceptionalities, can actually be the strongest. Diversity brings different perspectives to any discussion and study.

∅

Another writer who pays homage to the diversity in America through a musical metaphor is Walt Whitman (1904, 17) in his poem "I Hear America Singing." "I hear America singing, the varied carols I hear," Whitman proclaims and then continues to specify the people he hears, people from all walks of life.

The theme of this poem is most effectively revealed when the poem is performed by the many voices of a class, an activity that illustrates America singing. Many language arts teachers teach choral reading as a public speaking strategy. There are a variety of choral reading techniques:

- Solo: lines are read individually by different students.

- Unison: lines are read simultaneously by the entire class or by a certain number of students or by certain students (for example students can read together by row, by gender, by sides of the room, and so forth).

- Line-around: A line is read by one student or a small group, another reads the next line, and so on, going around the class.

- Echo: lines are read by one student or group and repeated by another, either immediately after, or a few beats behind, the first reader(s).

- Antiphonal: one line is read by a student or group and "answered" by another.

- Cumulative: one student or group reads a line; another student/ group joins in as each line is read, building in intensity.

- Volume, pitch, rate, and expression can also be orchestrated by the readers.

The teacher marks up copies of the poem or asks students to mark the poem in the most effective manner.

A powerful way to read the poem is for one student to read the first line. Then twelve different students, pairs, or small groups join in for each of the professions—mechanic, carpenter, mason, boatman, deckhand, shoemaker, hatter, woodcutter, plowboy, mother, young wife, girl—in line-around or cumulative reading, ending with the class in unison or echo. This is one example; the students can collaborate or small groups can perform it in diverse ways. In choral reading, the students hear the diversity and harmony in their voices.

Student #1: "I hear America singing,"
The entire class: "the varied carols I hear,"
Student pair #1: "Those of mechanics, each one singing his as it should be blithe and strong,"
Student pair #2: "The carpenter singing his as he measures his plank or beam,"

As a next step, the students can update and populate the poem with professions and people they know. Especially in current times, everyone may not have a profession, but teachers can point out that Whitman was focusing on "each singing what belongs to him or her and to none else."

It is a heartbreaking fact that not all our students see themselves accepted as a part of America. In 1925 Langston Hughes (1994, 46) wrote, "I, Too, Sing America" adding himself and all his "darker brothers" to the mix that is America and becoming a part of the puzzle. We want all our children to feel this acceptance—for themselves and for each other. Therefore, Hughes' poem is an important pairing with the Whitman poem.

Teachers need to discuss that Whitman, as well as our Founding Fathers, did not include all people, as we sometimes do not, and that, while Hughes laments his exclusion from American society, he recognizes that a change in American is imminent, that "they" will eventually see his worth and beauty and feel shame.

Hughes' phrase "darker brother" gives teachers a chance to talk about judging and being judged by appearances; accepting each other, such as the plant or the insect in the flower garden; and accepting ourselves. Children collect dandelions and violets—weeds, to some—for beautiful bouquets for their mothers. Langston Hughes' pride in his beauty comes though as we read the poem.

Students are likely not comfortable enough at this point to talk about their personal "darkness," but this is a good place for the language arts class to use literature and literary characters to discuss acceptance of image. Chapter 8 includes lists of books that focus on issues of personal acceptance.

After discussing diversity and the value of diversity in the abstract through literary works, teachers are ready to put this concept into practice through a whole class project in which each student contributes what he or she does best.

Whole-class projects can be designed to demonstrate that everyone has different talents, skills, and intelligences and, more importantly, that combining those talents in a collaborative work makes for a superior result. A representative example is the Home Front Fair, a project created for a humanities (language arts, social studies) class.

BUILDING COMMUNITY—
WHOLE-CLASS COLLABORATION

To begin to build a classroom community, an assignment which involves all members of the class in one project or, more manageably, in smaller parts of a whole-class project helps students to appreciate the divergent skills of their classmates as they become interdependent. Interdependency opens up possibilities of greater productivity, efficiency, and personal academic and affective growth as members of the group learn to collaborate in mutually beneficial ways.

The Home Front Fair, a Whole-Class Multiple-Intelligence Collaboration

To end a study of World War II or the 1940s, teachers can include an exploration of the American Home Front during World War II and its contribution to the overseas war effort. A Home Front inquiry can easily be structured to lend itself to inquiry that would be meaningful to the students, individually and as a group, and to bring the class together with a collaborative project that will highlight students in different roles based on their different interests, talents, and intelligences.

Assignments

1. Give students a brief overview of ways in which America was contributing to the war on the Home Front. Students will expand this information by conducting active research as a class.

2. Explain to students the theory of multiple intelligences, based on Howard Gardner's (2004) *Frames of Mind: The Theory of Multiple Intelligences*. The intelligences students possess: are musical-rhythmic, bodily-kinesthetic, visual-spatial, logical-mathematical, verbal-linguistic, naturalist, intrapersonal, and interpersonal. The students can use self-reflection, meta-cognition, and the Teele Inventory of Multiple Intelligences to help them determine their individual dominant intelligences.

3. To highlight each of these intelligences and allow students having each intelligence to play a significant part in the project, the class plans three Discovery Centers: a USO canteen, a live radio broadcast, and a general store. These centers would encompass the mainstream of American life as it related to the war and will highlight individual students' strengths and intelligences.

4. The students form the three groups and assign positions based on their dominant intelligences.

   a. A board composed of the chairperson for the fair, as well as the chairperson for each Discovery Center, is made up of those students with strong *interpersonal* talents.

   b. The USO canteen is comprised of a band and vocalists (*musical-rhythmic intelligence*) and dancers (*bodily-kinesthetic intelligence*).

   c. The radio broadcast team includes those students with strong *verbal-linguistic* interests.

   d. The general store incorporates those with *visual-spatial* strengths and the *logical-mathematical* students.

   e. Teachers should also plan a role for any student who is more *intrapersonal* and would prefer to work individually on something more reflective. These students, in their roles as fictitious World War II persons, could reflect on their lives, problems, concerns, hopes and dreams, and survival techniques with collages, scrapbooks, memento trunks, or newspaper articles to share with the guests. Even though they will not be members of a particular

Discovery Center, they will be collaborating in the whole-class project. They are working individually, not independently. However, usually by this time students have become so comfortable with another that they do not mind working together.

5. Over the next few weeks, using research and family and community sources, each group investigates the background for and creates its discovery center and plans a twenty-minute presentation for the Home Front Fair. Each group decides what was necessary for its Center and presentation.

   a. The USO canteen would require the research and creation of appropriate decorations, food, live music, vocal performances, and dancing, which utilize the skills of artists, musicians, dancers, bakers, and singers.

   b. The general store would be designed and built by those students sporting visual-spatial strengths, and may include such sections as a war bond booth, a fat-collecting station, and a gas station. In one class, a ration-coupon consumer activity was planned for the "customers" based on 1940s professional incomes and ration allowances, which kept the mathematicians busy.

   c. After the components of radio news shows are researched, a radio news broadcast for December 8, 1941, or another significant date, with timely reports on science and discoveries, sports, health, entertainment, and weather can be presented to a live audience, with appropriate wartime commercials incorporated.

6. In groups and individually, the students conduct the print and electronic research, adding interviews with relatives and community members. For the Home Front Fair, everything created, worn, said, and done should be based on research and cited on note cards if the teacher wishes to verify the research and teach research methods and skills.

7. District residents can be requested to supply artifacts for display and decoration.

As the groups plan their presentations and activities, students meet with a variety of teachers (language arts, music, home economics, art, social studies, math, and even a local dance teacher) when appropriate.

Students will need to divide responsibilities and work collaboratively in groups and as a class to coordinate all activities.

The Timeline of a Home Front Fair

In one school, the groups were given basic weekly plans. Week 1 was to conduct preliminary research to determine the group's twenty-minute activity and what was needed to create their Discovery Center: 1941 radio station studio, USO canteen, or general store and gas station.

For example, the USO canteen needed to research what a USO canteen might look like and what activities occurred there. Researchers discovered that canteens were places where soldiers went for live music, singers, dancing with local ladies, and refreshments. Students then decided to have the singers sing one song accompanied by the musicians, and the dancers would teach the visitors one dance of the time period. And they would buy or make appropriate food, which they learned to be donuts and coffee, at least at the canteen in our local area. Their next step was to research songs and dances of the era.

During the second week, students conducted actual in-depth research and began working on the activity. This canteen group found that their team's math teacher was proficient in swing dancing and their active research was learning how to swing dance with him. Because the math teacher was not always available for lessons, a local dance teacher donated her time.

The singers and musicians researched songs, went through printed music, listened to CDs, and determined a song they could both play and sing; they then worked with their band and choral directors. This group also researched refreshments served, mainly by interviewing community senior citizens.

The third week was spent researching, building, and decorating the canteen; planning their twenty-minute activity; and creating "props" for the activity. The dancers made numbered footprints which they attached to the floor, the singers and musicians rehearsed, everyone researched clothing to be worn (USO armbands and stocking lines painted up the back of the "women's" legs), and they made table cloths and recreated art work for the canteen walls.

While the timelines of some groups varied, and research, construction, and rehearsal activities were recursive, this was the general plan. They were fortunate enough to have the library and the assistance of the librarian during class period for the three weeks; therefore, the teacher could keep her eye on, and consult with, all groups.

The night of the Home Front Fair, relatives and community members were invited so that students could share their in-depth research, creations, and presentations and the guests could share their personal World War II experiences with the students. Visitors brought war memorabilia for a special display, which turned the spotlight briefly on the significance of community members. During the fair, each group performed its presentation as the guests rotated among the Discovery Centers.

The values of this project are numerous and varied. Besides the predictable reading, writing, speaking, listening, and research skills, they include

- Acquisition of a sense of family and community history.
- Interaction and communication with various generations of the local community.
- Building upon the learning of others and the diverse intelligences of other fellow students.
- Practicing collaborative learning strategies.

Following the presentation, in one class a student wrote on his project self-evaluation, "Through researching, I learned that it is in the best interest of the researcher that he use as many resources as possible. It is also beneficial if a variety of sources is used. I found that one of the best resources is other people."

Another participant wrote, "From talking to my parents and relatives, I learned how wise and useful they really are. Many times I called my grandfather for information about things I wasn't around to see. I learned about my own relatives who served in the war. I learned that my great uncle, who I have never met but had seen in pictures, was somewhat of a hero, and he received medals and commendations."

Yet a third made an additional point: "Many of the things I learned came from other classmates." And a fourth student made the following observation: "The most surprising thing was what somebody can do if you give them [*sic*] time. Also what a group can do if they work together."

By working as a group based on individual, divergent intellectual and experiential strengths, each student was able to more vividly, and more purposefully, comprehend the content and fulfill the assignment. What the students actually learned was the value of others, and that those whose knowledge, experience, and skills were most different from theirs were the most valuable.

As part of the curriculum, this project covers standards in reading, writing, speaking, listening, researching, World War II history, state history, and technology. The list could continue on and on.

CREATING PUZZLES: OTHER WHOLE-CLASS IDEAS FOR CONTENT AREA CLASSES

Obviously every class does not lend itself to a Home Front Fair, and many teachers already include collaborative projects in their curriculum. However, it is of primary importance that any such project or activity requires the cooperative efforts of the divergent skills, talents, intelligences, and cultures that make each student an essential piece of the puzzle.

As author Tom Robbins (2003) wrote, "Our similarities bring us to a common ground; our differences allow us to be fascinated by each other." Teachers will find students absolutely fascinated by the skills, knowledge, background, and talents that each brought to the table.

The challenge for teachers is in creating the activity. They will need to think about different strengths their students might have and create an assignment that would involve every type of student. A class could create a Civil War Fair with different activities; turn a Shakespearean play or any novel or short story into a musical in the manner of *Oliver!*; use music and movement as a background for a depiction of the planets of the solar system; or create a "math-letics" activity day with some events based on music, some on movement, some on reflection, some on individual activities, and some on cooperative activities.

In any content area, students can write a play and add music and dancing à la *1776*: *The Phantom of the Ecosystem, A Funny Thing*

Happened on the Way to _____ *Class,* or *Geometry World,* to name a few examples.

The merit of these whole-class projects or activities is the realization that, as Handlin (1986, 6) observed, through the collaboration of divergent people, individual students "enriched the culture of the whole with their own special contributions."

It is advantageous to also build community across the academic team and make each student a part of the "puzzle." Community-building can involve scheduling a whole team or grade activity during the first half of the academic year.

For this type of activity students can divide themselves by their talents, skills, intelligences, and content-area proficiencies or proclivities. They are then teamed for a multifaceted activity, such as an academic, trivia, and sports combination contest, with teams comprised of students with divergent strengths and abilities. Through the interdependence needed to compete as a team, students will become acquainted with the abilities of their peers and discover the value of everyone as "part of the puzzle."

4

SMALL-GROUP COLLABORATION

Years ago the "ideal" classroom was set up on the advice of veteran teachers as "five rows of six, *not* six rows of five." The theory was to keep the students farther apart so it was harder for them to talk to each other and harder for them to copy from each other.

WORKING TOGETHER

Currently, many teachers position their students purposely to allow for collaboration. An effective arrangement can still be six rows of five *but* with the six rows across arranged in pairs. Three sets of pairs across work well because everyone can quickly find a partner to talk to, collaborate with, and even "copy" from (when warranted). Students also can quickly form triads by separating the middle pair of seats, and they can fashion quartets by joining the partnership in front or behind them.

Students are aware of when *not* to collaborate (tests); at those times they can easily move the rows farther apart into single rows. Classroom arrangements can vary from day to day and class to class, and for some activities students may sit in small circles or rectangles of five or six. For variety, partnerships need not always be identical, but seat placement demonstrates to students whether collaboration and teamwork is valued as a learning tool.

Social skills as well as content skills need to be modeled and taught. When working in collaborative groups, students need to be taught how to discuss and listen and about what to talk—content, not Friday night's movie.

It may take some teachers a while to understand the merit of collaboration. *Isn't it cheating if they work together?* As teachers we need to keep in mind the ultimate goals of our classes: academic—*all* students learning—and social—all students learning to work with others. And the best way to accomplish both is through collaboration and cooperation, students supporting students. Most adolescents and especially middle grade students are very social, and therefore, teachers might as well exploit that trait. Classroom collaboration also helps the shy students to become a part of a group and it is a real-world objective—more and more businesses and professions are being organized as teams.

MAKING STONE SOUP

In the folktale "Stone Soup," three hungry soldiers come to a village to beg some food. Since food is scarce, the villagers insist they have none. The men place some stones in a pot with some water and proceed to boil the water, claiming they are making stone soup. One by one, the villagers each bring a food item to add to the pot so that they can share in the soup. As each villager brings a vegetable, some rice, or a little meat, the soup becomes richer and more abundant until the entire village is able to dine quite well.

Many cultures have a variant of this tale because it contains a universal message. When each person has something to add, no matter how little, it makes the end product superior.

The previous chapter presented whole-class projects in which class members each see themselves as essential parts of a puzzle or orchestra or garden or whatever the metaphor for the class. Many times it is more beneficial to work in smaller groups within the class where each person's contribution is more crucial as fewer students pool their resources and talents. These projects need to be designed so that one person cannot do all, or even most, of the work or fulfill all the tasks, so that students of a variety of skills and abilities are essential to the project. This strategy is in keeping with Aristotle: "The whole is greater than the sum of its parts."

SMALL-GROUP COLLABORATION: THE TOWN PROJECT

One sample project that teachers across the country have implemented, and appears from former students to be most memorable, is the Town Project (Roessing 2004, 18–24). In this project, groups of five or six students design a town of any type—a city, village, island, or hamlet. They determine the size, location, and topography of the town; its main industry and commercial businesses; and the more important governmental, religious, and private institutions and buildings—schools, hospitals, town centers, roads and highways, waterways, recreation centers, and so forth.

Together, they map the town, planning the location and size of commercial, industrial, and residential districts, and construct a chart of any vital statistics they can think of, such as population, religions, professions, income, government officials, and indigenous animals.

As the next step, town members draft a description and history of their town, only limited by their imaginations and knowledge base. The talents and intelligences needed are multiple—artists, mathematicians, scientists, researchers, writers, statisticians, geographers, cartographers, and simple observers of their own towns. This is a classic case in which many heads are better than one, as students bounce their ideas off one another.

Next, the town creators populate their town with its more interesting citizens, and each student adopts a citizen and makes him or her the protagonist of an original short story. Students can brainstorm plots together, or not, but when the drafts are completed, they serve as a response group for each other's stories. Since these are stories of *their* town, everyone has a vested interest.

Here again, a wealth of diversity adds—some students are better at writing, some at revision, some at editing, some at details and fact-checking, others at having an ear for authentic dialogue, and others at punctuating that dialogue. Everyone has a hand in each story since the stories, as well as the map, chart, description, and history, will be published in a book with the stories of the class's other towns, and each class member will receive a copy.

Adolescents learn new things about their classmates. They are amazed that Amber can draw so well and that John lived out West and knows how the people speak. Tom's father works in human resources and can advise what different professions earn; Jenna's talent is planning scale models and measuring; Carla cannot spell well, but she knows how to write dialogue; and each town knows it has one of the best writers in the class.

As the final component of the project, the class listens to taped radio shows, studies sound effects, and chooses one of their town stories to turn into a radio script for a twenty-minute live radio show. Two students work on turning the story into a script, two write commercials featuring the town's products and businesses, and one works on reproducing the sound effects being written into the script.

Towns perform the radio show with each person reading a part in the main story and the commercials. Teachers have found the quietest child in the class to be able to speak with the funniest accents. Ryan reproduced car chase sounds so perfectly that the audience ducked as the police car "came around the bends," and there were those who wrote theme songs for their shows and played them on keyboards. Every year in classes there will be students who completely surprise their peers by sharing hidden talents that enhance their group project.

Taking the Town Project into the twenty-first century, one teacher had students create digital stories and podcast their radio shows.

This project is delineated in detail because it illustrates that even a writing project brings out the value of those students who may be weak or reluctant writers. This type of project allows for a divergence of skills and talents, and each town will highlight different talents. Some will produce intricate maps, drawn to scale with elaborate buildings, a variety of streets and residences, and a complex topography, while some will have individual plotlines that merge into another's story, and some will have catchy radio show theme songs that students are humming for weeks as they laugh about Sarah's multitude of accents.

The Town Project is adaptable to social studies where students can recreate historic places and events and tell the stories of the people—famous or fictitious—who lived then. One social studies teacher decided to have her students create towns at the beginning of the year and chronicle the changes that occur as the towns progress through their study of history throughout the year.

In science class, the habitats can be situated in divergent ecosystems or even on different planets with inhabitants of a variety of species. In foreign language classes, the towns can be part of the cultures being studied. In a mathematics class, various geometric shapes could house communities or the communities could house geometric shapes as characters in the manner of the novel *Flatland: A Romance of Many Dimensions* (Abbott 2005).

SMALL-GROUP COLLABORATION: OTHER PROJECTS ACROSS THE CURRICULUM

Another activity in which students of differing abilities can equally contribute is the assignment of small-group newspapers that focus on material in a textbook chapter or the setting and plot of a novel. The gregarious adolescent can conduct a "people poll," while the serious writer drafts the hot news story. The reflective student writes a "Dear Abby" column, while the weaker writers might have ideas for comic strips based on the information to be imparted, or as an avid comic book collector, the best ideas of how to convert the text into a comic strip; or they might possess the best computer skills. Some of the least academically motivated students have taught their teachers how to use technology to produce a more effective product.

A different type of endeavor allowing students to showcase their individual talents in a mathematics class might be that of creating a business—finances, creating a product, market surveys, advertising (persuasive writing and art), bookkeeping . . . The list can extend indefinitely.

Another quality that any adolescent can contribute to a group is perspective. Each of us sees things from an individual point of view; sharing those perspectives makes the view 360 degrees. Any topic can benefit by the multiple voices of individuals: students reading an article and writing their responses as poems, drawing them as pictures . . . As long as there is no "correct" answer expected, all students can feel they contributed equally.

In homeroom, group projects may comprise of door decorating for various occasions and holidays. Door decorating can be a school-wide, grade-wide, or team-wide contest or just for homerooms that want attractive, personalized entrances. As knowledge of their interests and skills emerge, homeroom students divide themselves into the idea creators, the designers, and the decorators.

Some students can collaborate in creating and drafting the design, a few can bring in supplies, some cut and paste, and others actually hang the decorations. And then there are the critics. Even though this could be considered a whole-class project, students tend to divide the project into smaller segments. Students who are not present for the door decorating—rehearsals, absenteeism—can extend the decorating to the rest of the classroom to further the theme.

Again, students who do not know each other's strengths discover how valuable divergent skills can be within this community-building activity. And of course, everyone likes to celebrate or commemorate with a decorated door.

✆

In his Intergroup Contact Theory, Gordon Allport (1954) held that positive effects of intergroup contact occur only in situations marked by four key conditions:

- Equal group status within the situation.
- Common goals.
- Intergroup cooperation.
- The support of authorities, law, or custom [in this case, the teacher].

The activities outlined in this chapter contain all four conditions.

NO WINNERS, NO LOSERS: COOPERATIVE GAME PLAYING

One way to achieve an understanding of collaboration and mutual respect is through games or activities that have no winners and, therefore, no losers. Chapter 3 discussed how each student can become a piece of the puzzle by something unique he or she can offer; activities in chapter 4 build on that notion with interdependency and collaboration to improve the group dynamic or a group enterprise. Taking this a step further is the notion that there not always need to be winners and losers, that everyone is worthy of respect for whatever his or her contribution may be, and that play can also be cooperative.

There are classic games many of us have played in childhood that have no winners or losers; these are the games that emphasize participation, challenge, fun, and just playing together. Some that come to mind are Statues, Leapfrog, and Who Stole the Cookies from the Cookie Jar? Even Tag reverses the winner-loser concept because the tagged person takes control of the game by becoming "it." In some games, such as hopscotch and jump rope, the most one can lose is one's turn—temporarily. These games do not end when someone wins; they end only when the players become tired of playing the game.

The New Games Book (Fluegelman 1976) emphasizes the concept of cooperative play. The book's subtitle is *Play Hard, Play Fair, Nobody Hurt*. Although the slogan most likely refers to physical harm, games without winners also go a long way to making sure that nobody will be hurt emotionally. And though some of the new games are competitive, it is inherent in the rules that players are free to change sides or opt out— and then back in—at any time; therefore, no one actually has to lose.

But how can teachers rationalize game playing in school? Many middle schools still have some sort of recess or lunch break time; unfortunately, this may be a time where students divide into groups or cliques rather than come together. It also is the time that much bullying takes place. Researchers in Canada spent hundreds of hours taping playgrounds. During this time, they observed an episode of bullying every eight minutes.

In the ABC News Special "The 'In' Crowd and Social Cruelty" (2002), professor of psychology Wendy Craig explained, "Recess for them [kids who are constantly picked on] is the most terrifying moment of the day."

Research shows that the majority of low-level aggression in the school occurs in *unstructured* school settings, such as on the playground during recess. A team led by psychologist Stephen Leff collaborated with Philadelphia school administrators, teachers, parents, and playground supervisors to design and implement a playground-based intervention. Their rationale was twofold:

- The primary concern indicated by the school partners was to establish a socialized recess program whereby children would play together more cooperatively, with less aggression and rough play.
- A second issue was to promote better interaction among children of different ethnic backgrounds (Leff and Munro, 2009).

Over the course of several months, the researchers and playground supervisors collaborated weekly to develop a structured and engaging recess program, through learning fun and engaging activities, active monitoring strategies, and successful techniques to handle aggressive behaviors. A year later, the research team conducted observations and found

- That structured and cooperative games played during school recess can have a strong impact on increasing childhood prosocial behaviors and decreasing behaviors found to lead to aggression and bullying (e.g., high levels of rough physical play).
- That "further, the role of active supervision among adults on the playground had beneficial effects, especially in promoting positive interactions among youth of diverse cultures."

Leff points out that this type of structure is even more important in low-income areas where there are less playground equipment and supervision. However, it is precisely in those low income neighborhoods that many middle schools have no playground equipment, and students are left to their own devices for entertainment (Leff and Munro 2009).

Collaborative games do not require expensive specialized equipment, just safe space (fields and gymnasiums), but they do require leadership and supervision. However, the leadership need not come exclusively from adults. Training students to act as *effective* leaders is also a positive way for building self-respect and respect among peers.

A rational for using cooperative games to reduce bullying is found on the New Games website (http://www.inewgames.com/newgamesbenefits .htm): "The games are a great way to mix people of all kinds, giving them a friendly, fun way of relating to each other. This gives those who are normally picked on and those who do the bullying an opportunity to interact with others, including each other. It's hard to have negative feelings when everyone is laughing and having fun together."

Successfully testing this assertion, Dale LeFevre, director of New Games International, has given New Games workshops in thirty-two countries, including with Jews and Arabs in the early 1980s in Israel; with mixed races in apartheid South Africa; with Protestants and Catholics in the early 1980s in Northern Ireland; and with Croats, Serbs, and Muslims in 1993–94 in Croatia.

For those middle schools that do not have a recess period, many of these games are appropriate for inside during homeroom time or outside as a whole-team activity during a team time. Teams can hold an activity day or activity hours a few times a year as team-building occasions. Students who work together at games take that collaboration into the classroom, building the *we*. The better adolescents come to know each other through working together, the more they respect each other.

Resources for cooperative games are listed in chapter 8.

Teamwork, collaboration, and cooperation makes a hearty beef vegetable stew from stone soup. As John Lennon stated, quoting Yoko Ono, "A dream you dream alone is only a dream. A dream you dream together is reality" (Sheff 2000, 16).

5

EVERYONE IS AN EXPERT: VALUING DIVERSITY AND CELEBRATING INDIVIDUALITY

The class was reading "The House Guest" by Paul Darcy Boles. In the story, Bridgie, a young girl from Northern Ireland, is staying with an American family and becomes agitated when she hears a car backfire. The class discussed why this was so. When a car backfires, it sounds like a gunshot, and where Bridgie comes from, gunshots are daily occurrences.

As the discussion progressed, some of the students looked blank as if not aware of the sound of backfiring. Realized she hadn't heard any cars backfire in a number of years, the teacher ruminated aloud, asking what she thought was a rhetorical question, "Why haven't I heard a car backfire lately?" when a hand shot into the air. It was Ellen.

Ellen went into a long, technical explanation about why cars no longer backfire. Noting the class's surprise that someone could actually answer the question, Ellen revealed that her father is an auto mechanic and she spends a lot of time helping him in the shop. Ellen instantly became the class automobile expert. Whenever students wrote stories that involved cars, they went to Ellen for accuracy and advice. They also found that her automotive knowledge was transferrable to incidents in other stories, those the students read and those they wanted to write.

Ellen became not just a classmate but a valuable resource in reading and writing workshops. Ellen's information was passed on in every reading of "The House Guest" afterward. Ellen left the classroom, but her expertise remained.

Ellen's guidance demonstrates that every student knows something—or at least more than others—about something. Teachers need to help students identify and appreciate their areas of expertise or topics in which they are already interested and, therefore, would like to develop some expertise.

UNCOVERING EXPERTISE

Teachers can assemble a questionnaire, noting their own personal examples as models:

What I Know a Lot About

from family: diamond quality (Father), soap opera plotlines (Mom) cooking terms (son), forestry issues (daughter), legal terms (husband)
from friends: photography terms, Southern plantings
from hobbies: leatherworking techniques
from reading: anorexia, Holocaust, adolescent literature
from experience: healthy eating, being a mom, twirling a baton
from trips or vacations: Italy, Spain, Budapest

Teachers next ask students to add suggestions to the list. Some add innovative categories:

from school classes: German, real estate law
from jobs or volunteer activities: telephone switchboards, planning relay races
from sports: golf, racquetball, tennis
from television: crime labs, plot structures of sitcoms, recipes

Figure 5.1 shows a sample chart. Another way to organize the questionnaire is by topics (figure 5.2). At this point, teachers can allow the students to brainstorm the remainder of the list.

What I Know a Lot About

FROM:	TEACHER EXAMPLE	STUDENT RESPONSES
Parents or relatives:		
Friends:		
Hobbies:		
Reading:		
Experience:		
Trips or vacations:		
School classes:		
Jobs/volunteer activities:		
Sports:		
Television or movies:		

Figure 5.1.

What I Know a Lot About

People: *Nelson Mandela, Katherine Paterson, camp counselors, foresters, lawyers*

Places: *Adirondacks, small towns, New York City, Savannah, Venice*

Animals: *Australian shepherds, Shetland sheepdogs*

Things: *jewelry, nutrition*

Sports and activities: *golf, acting, weight lifting, tennis*

Figure 5.2.

Classes can discover quite a lot about each other, and students find new allies with whom to pursue learning (and hobbies). Some students will gain new respect for fellow students, those they may have considered "losers" or "others." It may seem that everyone has a secret life.

In one classroom, a student showed ferrets in competitions; another was a skateboarding champion. The quiet girl in the back of the room had a black belt in karate, and two students had snakes as pets and now someone with whom to discuss the trials and tribulations of snake feeding. Someone even had an uncle in the circus. Parents were in bands and in professions many students had not heard of. Two students had vacationed in the same place for years.

Besides the affective and, therefore, classroom community advantages (see chapter 4), the class can brainstorm topics in which students can ask for support or background information when reading. They can also target topics writers can now write about with more accuracy for expository writings or for use for settings, plots, and characters for narrative fiction.

Kerry admitted that she had started a story that was to take place in the circus but couldn't continue because it did not seem accurate or "real." Bobby offered Kerry his uncle's email address, and "The Tightrope Walker" was published in the classroom.

Many students originally assume they have no areas of special knowledge; these are the ones who feel they never have anything to offer in school. However, after discussing the questionnaire, Sam volunteered that he knew a great deal about the court system and how a courtroom is designed. The teacher did not inquire about the origin of his knowledge, but when the class decided to write and perform a trial based on a novel, Sam, who had never willingly taken part in any language arts project, was the staging man. He even went back to the book to give advice about placement of people and furniture and about what characters—bailiff, court reporter—were needed to make the courtroom more realistic.

As classmates' strengths are noted for the class, teachers will discover that students who excel in other content areas can be tapped for assistance, not only in those courses, but also in language arts writing. One class found that Bob could be consulted about historical dates and that any of the math-inclined students could assist with using logic and statistics to ground argumentation and debate. With John's and Sarah's knowledge and interest in science, their classmates could now write science fiction, and they could supply background information for reading science fiction texts. They were so interested in science that they were willing to conduct research in almost any scientific area to retain their "expert" status.

When writing books for a Holocaust unit, those students who had already studied some German were of assistance in making the dialogue more realistic. Even if their German grades were not the best, they were familiar enough with the German dictionary or knew the German teacher better than the others and could ask her for information.

The repertoire expands as collaboration grows. A story no longer is "his" or "hers"; it is "our" story. There is no work by "others" as the barter system grows. "If you help create statistics for my commercial, I will help you find out boating terms for your island story. My uncle and aunt own a marina." Even though students can be working on individual writings, and, in some cases, readings, they can work together.

It is not the collaboration model discussed in chapter 4 but even more authentic collaboration—those between specialists—as used in today's business world. Students will be seeing each other as valuable resources and, therefore, valuable people, especially during workshops.

PEER REVIEW AND EDITING FOR
WRITINGS ACROSS THE CURRICULUM

With the new core curriculum standards, teachers need to conduct more writing across the curriculum in all content areas. While some content area teachers are hesitant or actually uncomfortable about *teaching writing*, rather than assigning writing, especially in the revision and editing stages, they can allow their class "experts" to take over. All students study the language arts and writing; therefore, they may be more familiar, or more up-to-date, with writing techniques and strategies than even their content area teachers.

Everyone is an expert on something. When students have been together for a few classes or a few grade levels, teachers may notice that students join certain groups to review particular types of writing, be it expository or narrative, an essay, or a poem. Teachers may observe students also going to specific students for assistance or advice on certain elements of writing (good leads, transition phrases, deleting unnecessary information) or for editing help (commas, semicolons, spelling).

There may be perceived experts in commas, in sentences structure, in spelling. Sometimes it is like watching a choreographed dance as students seek feedback on their writings. In some circumstances, they know each other better than their current teacher knows them, and many times they know who the specialist is they need.

Teachers can capitalize on this practice of review and editing experts. Adults identify their writing strengths and weaknesses, and students can also. At the beginning of the year, teachers can ask students to fill out a questionnaire, identifying their writing strengths so that they could use their "specialties" in assisting classmates. Teachers should remind them that they do not have to be perfect; they only have to be better than those peers seeking help.

For editing help, classes can have Grammar Gurus, Commas-after-Clause Consultants, Knowing-When-to-Spellcheck Whizzes, and Proofreading Prodigies. For revision support, there can be the Attention-Getting Lead Aides, Descriptive-Adjective Authorities, Conclusions Consultants, Specific-Detail Developers, and Idea Instigators.

Other experts are Website Wonders (those who know the best ways to traverse the World Wide Web). With enough categories, teachers can help all class members find strengths to share.

UNCOVERING EXPERTISE ACROSS THE CURRICULUM

Experts do not only exist in language arts classes. In social studies there are always those students who have some attraction to, and therefore knowledge of, particular historical periods, such as World War I or colonial America, or of war or battles in general; and there are those who love weapons and airplanes. Teachers can direct these interests into "authority areas" in their classes. And expertise does not only relate to topics.

There are students who can perform the computations for timeline design and scale maps; there are frequently skilled map readers, time-line drawers, and those who have an aptitude or who have developed the skills necessary to interpret and explain graphs. In math there are students who have mastery in shapes, in sizes, in drawing graphs, and in the various math processes. "Need a square root? Make an appointment with Sean."

Each subject area has its own fields of expertise, and there are always those areas that crisscross curricular lines: the illustrators, the vocabulary enthusiasts, the organizers, and those who are knowledgeable about what supplies are needed or about negotiating with others. Getting to know students and a little teacher creativity can turn every classroom into a room full of specialists; conferring with the other teachers in a grade-level team can yield yet more experts across the curriculum. Once the science teacher knew of Ellen's knowledge of motors and machinery, she could also be consulted in the physics unit of science class.

To let others in the class recognize the areas of expertise, the class can post a list on the bulletin board or students can make signs for their desks, or business cards, just like real professionals. Students can write ads for a class or team newspaper or print coupons that other students can remit for advice or assistance in our mission to make students value themselves and others (figure 5.3).

This process could stretch across the academic team. Many times a student will feel more comfortable going to a student in another science class for science help rather than to those classmates he faces each day. Or possibly the student with the required expertise is not enrolled in the same class.

ACADEMIC HELP COUPON

Good for one EDITING SESSION with
Sarah Smith, HR 24
Redeemable during Homeroom Period Mondays

CHARGE: one reciprocal session
in one of client's areas of academic/athletic expertise

Figure 5.3.

Through these conversations and activities, students learn to value themselves and others. They appreciate that everyone can be an expert in some areas, and at times that expertise benefits others. This is just another step moving adolescents toward the goal of valuing diversity.

6

MAKING EVERY DAY MULTICULTURAL DAY: STUDYING AND VALUING ALL CULTURES

Jen was leafing through a *National Geographic*. She came across a photograph of a woman with a neck stretched by a stack of neck rings. "That's different," she mused. The teacher had been hearing that term, *different*, and its counterparts *unusual, interesting,* and *unique,* more and more often in the classroom. She smiled, remembering that at the beginning of the year as students encountered different cultures and time periods in their study of human rights, the word heard most often was *weird*.

Different is, well, just different, not necessarily a word with positive or negative connotations; *weird*, however, in teen-speak, is a highly negative quality. How did the students get to this point, the point where they expressed interest and even understanding, rather than judgment? Through a year of focusing on similarities and acknowledging the value of diversity, learning about themselves as a class or a homeroom and also studying many other cultures beyond their small community.

MULTICULTURAL STUDIES

Many schools, even many districts, hold a Multicultural Day or a Multicultural Week. It is a time to celebrate other cultures, their foods, and perhaps their crafts and clothing. Educators need to be careful that such celebrations don't put the focus on others as being *other,* seeing them as "them." Students cook, bring in other foods, and wear other clothing, and it is a one-time event.

In this setting, it would be more beneficial to illustrate and discuss the similarities of foods in various cultures and, in many cases, that variations are based on availability of ingredients in the region—many of the differences are a matter of environment, not people. Enclosing fillings in dough is a widespread culinary tradition: pierogi, pot stickers, dumplings, knishes, ravioli, gyoza, empanadas. It would be more advantageous to have students make or bring in foods from different cultures that are similar and investigate the reason for the differences. There is at least one series of picture books, *Everybody Cooks Rice, Everybody Bakes Bread, Everybody Brings Noodles,* and *Everybody Serves Soup* by Norah Dooley, that exemplifies this point (see also the Reading Resources list in chapter 8).

However, a more constructive acknowledgment of the benefits of multiculturalism would focus on including the study of culture, not on one day or one week, but throughout the year as an integral part of the curriculum. Commonly, multicultural activities are confined to multi-ethnic studies. Culture is more than ethnicity; culture also encompasses nationality, race, socioeconomic status, gender, exceptionality, religion, and even age group and geographical location.

MULTICULTURAL LITERATURE

There are many ways to expose adolescents to multiculturalism in the broadest sense. In language arts class, teachers can ascertain that, instead of studying "multicultural literature" as a separate genre, the literature read, whether assigned by the teacher or self-selected by the students, are written by authors and contain characters and settings of divergent cultures in their broadest sense. The school media center and, even more important, classroom libraries should contain a cultural assortment, and teachers should be familiar with "multicultural" books.

In reading workshop where frequently students choose their own reading materials, teachers can request that readers keep a diversity chart (figure 6.1) so they become conscious of reading books about divergent

Culture		Text 1	Text 2	Text 3	Text 4	Text 5
Ethnicity / Nationality	Characters					
	Setting					
	Author					
Race	Characters					
	Author					
Gender	Protagonist					
	Author					
Socioeconomic Status	Characters/Setting					
	Author					
Exceptionality	Characters					
	Author					
Religion	Characters					
	Author					
Geography	Setting					
	Author					
Age Group	Characters					
Date Written	Author					

Figure 6.1.

cultures, whether through the authors, characters, or settings. A bibliography of young adult multicultural texts, picture books, poetry, short stories, essays, nonfiction, novels, and memoirs is included in chapter 8.

MULTICULTURALISM ACROSS THE CURRICULUM

In content area classes, it is imperative to note contributions made by scientists, mathematicians, historians, artists, musicians, sports figures, and others of diverse cultures as well as contributions made within various cultures. Young students tend to think that whatever they study originated in the United States and, unless they study the specific race or ethnicity of the inventor, by default he, or she, is a member of the predominant culture. Students have noticed and questioned the fact that they only study Martin Luther King Jr. or other African Americans during Black History Month, or focus on women's valuable contributions during Women's History Month, or read Gary Soto's writings during Hispanic Heritage Month. It may seem that studies of those people who are members of minority cultures are based solely on the fact that they are part of the celebrated culture or take place at a time reserved by presidential decree or the Library of Congress for the study of that culture, no matter how valuable or extensive their contributions to society as a whole.

It is interesting to adolescents to investigate the origins of inventions or discoveries. Sometimes the nationality, race, gender, age, and even the economic status of originator are complete surprises. According to Internet sources, coffee was first brewed in Yemen around the nineteenth century. The word *algebra* comes from the title of a Persian mathematician's famous nineteenth-century treatise, built on the roots of Greek and Hindu systems.

Greece had the first showers; Egypt is credited with the calendar, and China with creating gunpowder, printing, stirrups, and the compass. Alfred Nobel of Sweden (and Nobel Prize fame) first created dynamite. And India is the first "home" of buttons, iron, and dentistry. In mathematics class, tracing the origins of the zero would be a multicultural, or at least a multiethnic and multitemporal, puzzle.

Instead of celebrating Martin Luther King Day, students could celebrate a Human Rights Leaders' Day. Indeed, instead of taking away any attention from Reverend King, students can see him as one in a long line of activists throughout history and around the world, which should make his work even more valuable as students focus more on the work than the particular time and place and person. This type of activity also brings home that there are social justice issues and human rights heroes in all cultures.

COMPARING CULTURES: CINDERELLA AROUND THE WORLD

One cultural study conducted by many teachers at various grade levels and in a variety of curricular areas involves the Cinderella fairy tale, variants of which have been traced throughout the globe and to different ethnic and socioeconomic groups within continents and countries. By presenting authentic information about the geography, environment, government, family structure, food, clothing, class system, rituals, and values of a culture, folktales help children better understand cultures of diverse times and places, acknowledge their interrelatedness, and develop an appreciation for the customs and beliefs of different peoples.

Most Americans are familiar with Perrault's French *Cendrillon* (1697) and possibly the Grimm's *Aschenputtel* (1812), but there are more than fifteen hundred variants of the Cinderella tale recorded from cultures throughout the world. All contain common elements, or *motifs*, but are different in their reflection of the peoples—the customs, traditions, beliefs, and environments—from which they come. Therefore, the study of Cinderella becomes a comparative examination of cultures—their similarities and differences.

Even though evidence of a multitude of European variants has been recorded, it is believed that the earliest version of this story was the ninth-century Chinese tale *Yeh-Shen* (hence, the foot-and-shoe test which is common to the majority of variants). Besides the numerous European versions, there are varieties of the tale in most Asian cultures, as well as in North and South America, Africa, the Middle East, and post-Soviet states.

The following collaborative learning projects in which students—in all three middle grade levels and in both social studies and language arts classes—read, studied, and then compared Cinderella variants were created as a part of cultural studies. In the basic lesson plan, students read variants of the Cinderella story.

In a language arts class, students individually read self-selected variants; it was not significant which culture the tales represented because readers would then compare aspects of the twenty-four different cultures, first grouping by geographical area and then by criteria that they generated. In language arts, students were primarily concerned with analyzing whatever they gleaned from the tales themselves: setting, characters, conflicts, decisions, resolutions, purpose or theme, and how the individual folk tale motifs were handled.

In social studies classes, the class focused on one geographical area or continent; each group collaboratively read a variant from a different ethnic culture within that continent. For example, if the class was studying Asia, one group might read *Lily and the Wooden Bowl*, a Japanese Cinderella version, while another read *Jouanah*, a Hmong variant, and other groups read *Kao and the Golden Fish* from Thailand, *The Brocaded Slipper* from Vietnam, and *Abadeha* from the Philippines. If a teacher wishes to stress differences with national cultures, one group can read *Abadeha*, the Muslim variant, while another read the Tagalog version, *Maria*.

In other social studies classes, teachers assigned each group of students to collaboratively read a variant from a different geographical area: Europe, Asia, post-Soviet states, Africa, Middle East, and the United States. In the more advanced classes, each member of the group might read a different variant from that area.

The Lesson Plan

    I.   Goals:
        1. For students to become aware of, and knowledgeable about, other cultures.
        2. For students to appreciate the similarities and differences of various cultures.
        3. For students to appreciate the folktales of different cultures.
        4. For students to become aware of their own culture.

   II.   Objectives:
        1. Students will be able to list and explain some customs, beliefs, values, and environments of other cultures.

2. Students will be able to explain how their Cinderella tale fits the elements of both a folktale and a fairytale.
3. Students will be able to list the motifs of a Cinderella tale and that of at least two tales.
4. Students will be able to compare/contrast cultures.

III. Skills:
Reading, writing, speaking, listening, researching, comparing, and contrasting.

IV. Prerequisites:
Lesson on folktales.

V. Materials:
- *Cinderella* and one variant per student or per group and motif chart (figure 6.2).
- Optional: story map, research worksheet, sets-props-costumes worksheet, scriptwriting worksheet.

VI. Lesson description and procedures:
Class 1:
The teacher introduces the characteristics of all folk tales and any additional characteristics unique to fairytales (magic).

Class 2:
The teacher lists the *motifs* specific to a Cinderella tale:
- Heroine or hero (a virtuous and good-hearted daughter/son).
- Lowly position (through the death of mother).
- Villains (stepmother and stepsiblings or siblings).
- Social occasion.
- Potential spouse (someone respected in the culture).
- Impossible task (assigned by the villain[s]).
- Magic agent (representing the dead mother).
- Magical clothing or objects.
- Identity test (shoe test in the majority of tales).
- Resolution.
- Punishment for the villains.

Teacher model:
- The Teacher reads or reviews the most familiar Cinderella variant, Perrault's *Little Glass Slipper* written in France in the 1690s, and the class fills out the motif chart.

- The teacher points out and the students add any information about the cultural beliefs, traditions, and environment of the French culture reflected in the story (king, ball, etc.).

Class 3:

- The teacher reads or tells—by acting it out or using a puppet theater—a Cinderella tale from another culture, such as the German *Aschenputtel*, written down by the Grimm brothers, or the Appalachian *Ashpet*, based on a variant originally from Scotland.
- Guided practice: the students collaboratively fill out the motif chart for this tale.

Class 4:

The class is divided into groups, and each group is given copies of one variant.

Group members are assigned roles:

- Reader.
- Recorder.
- Culture researcher.
- Materials handler/artist.
- Director.

The story is read aloud by the reader, while the other group members follow along silently in their copies.

The group fills out the third column of the motif chart, while the recorder makes an official group copy.

Class 5:

1. The class briefly discusses the various ways a story can be presented to others, such as a live play, recorded movie, puppet show, picture book in prose, or narrative poem.
2. Keeping in mind the possible choices of presentations, the group reads its tale a second time.
3. As the reader rereads,
   - The director makes sure that all are listening and doing their jobs and keeps track of time.
   - The recorder fills out a story map of plot events.

- The researcher notes any possible cultural references in the story to investigate (clothing, animals, government officials, social occasions, physical environment, chores, foods, customs, etc.).
- The materials handler/artist notes the scenes (settings) of the story and any objects that would be crucial to presenting the story as a play or to drawing illustrations.

Class 6:

The class reviews the different presentation options and the guidelines for each.

The groups decide on the presentation format that would best fit their tale and their talents.

They plan the presentation and outline writing (script or book) ideas and materials needed.

Classes 7–8:
- Researcher researches the culture of the variant to write an introduction to the culture and gathers photos or descriptions for the appropriate clothing, settings, and objects in the play or books.
- Recorder and reader write the script or the text.
- Materials handler/artist and director plan the props, sets, and costumes (for people or puppets); or artist draws and materials handler colors the illustrations for the book.

Classes 9–10:

Students read through their scripts, practice their cultural introductions, and construct the props, costumes, and sets or put their books together and practice their presentations, reducing or expanding to ten minutes.

Class 11 (and possibly 12):

Presentations and discussions
- Each group performs its skit or puppet show or reads its book for the class. (A document project lets the authors share their illustrations; if not available, the illustrations can be shared through transparencies or PowerPoint slides.)

- Motifs charts can be expanded to include a column for each variant. As the groups present their cultures, the audience can complete their charts and have a basis for a whole-class conversation about culture.

VII. Extension activity:
Students fill out a column on their Motif chart for their own contemporary culture and either individually or collaboratively in small groups write a modern Cinderella variant that reflects their environment, customs, traditions, and beliefs.

°Samples of the story map, sets-props-costumes worksheet, research worksheet, and scriptwriting worksheet, as well as a list of forty-five titles of variants from different countries, are included at the end of the chapter.

Using folklore as a strategy is extremely effective in guiding adolescents to question assumptions and open themselves to the value of diversity. Ben, a sixth grade student, was raptly watching the animated video version of *Yeh-Shen*. He had been in the group that read one of the Japanese variant. After the video, he turned and said in a pensive voice, "I would have expected the Chinese version of the story to be more like the Japanese version since they are both in Asia. I will have to research and find out why they are so different."

This is an example of inquiry, leading to interest, leading to more inquiry and self-motivated learning. Figures 6.3 and 6.4 provide scriptwriting and set directions, and the appendix provides a list of variants on the Cinderella tale.

Cinderella Folk Tale Motif Comparison Chart

MOTIF CHART	French	German	Group Variant	Our Community
Title	*Little Glass Slipper*			
Heroine	Cendrillon (Cinderella)			
Cause of Low Position	mother dies; father remarries			
Villains	stepmother and 2 stepsisters			
Social Occasion	ball			
Potential Spouse	Prince (royalty)			
Impossible Task	chores; no dress			
Magic Agent	fairy godmother			
Magical Clothing/Objects	coach; footmen; gown; glass slippers			
Identity Test	shoe fits (small feet)			
Resolution	marries Prince; in higher position			
Punishment for Villains	none			
CULTURAL environment	royalty: King, prince; ball			
CULTURAL traditions	class system			

Figure 6.2.

SCRIPT WRITING

Go through your story and mark where one scene ends and another begins.
A **SCENE** changes when the place or time of the action changes.

For each scene you write, you will need to:

1) Explain what happens in the scene (this should match the scene explanation written on your group "Sets, Props, Costumes" worksheet list);

2) Describe the **SET** (scenery = background picture) and list all **CHARACTERS**.

3) Each scene consists of
STAGE DIRECTIONS which tell the characters what to do; put in [brackets]; &
DIALOGUE (which tells the characters what to say).

PROPS (objects used by the characters) are underlined in the stage directions.

EXAMPLE:

1) **Scene 1** is when Cinderella's stepfamily is mean to her and orders her to do chores. Also, in that scene, the King's messenger delivers the invitation to the ball.
It takes place in the house, near the fireplace.

2) **SET**: inside a French-style HOUSE - living room with fireplace; GARDEN outside
CHARACTERS: Cinderella, 2 stepsisters, stepmother, King's messenger

3) [*Cinderella is sleeping on floor near fireplace; she is dressed in rags, with bare feet*]
Stepmother [*pointing to Cinderella*]: Get up, you lazy girl. I don't know why I agreed to marry your widowed father and take care of you.
Stepsister 1 [*handing mop to Cinderella*]: Clean the floor! You have gotten your cinders from the fire all over it. I don't want to ruin my new dress.
Cinderella: Yes, stepsister. [*Turning to audience*]: I never had to do all this work when my mother was alive.
Stepsister 2 [*holding out her hairbrush, whining*]: I need Cinderella to brush my hair.

[*Doorbell rings and Stepmother answers. The messenger is standing outside, a large invitation in his hand*]
Messenger [*unscrolling and reading invitation*]: Next week the King is holding a ball to find a suitable wife for his son. All the unmarried women in the kingdom are invited.

Now write your script:
Scene 1 is when _____

SET: _____

CHARACTERS: _____

(_____) _____:_____

_____

_____

_____

Figure 6.3.

CINDERELLA: SETS, PROPS, COSTUMES

EXAMPLE:

Scene 1 is when Cinderella's stepfamily order her to do chores and are mean to her.

It takes place in the house, near the fireplace

Background picture needed fireplace and room of house.

Character	Costume	Prop(s)
Cinderella	rags and dirt	mop
Stepmother & sisters	fancy dresses or skirts	hand mirror

Now make your list - make sure that your scene description matches the Script.

Scene _____ is when _____

It takes place _____

Background picture needed _____

Character	Costume	Prop(s)

SCENE _____ is when _____

It takes place _____

Background picture needed _____

Character	Costume	Prop(s)

SCENE _____ is when _____

It takes place _____

Background picture needed _____

Character	Costume	Prop(s)

Figure 6.4.

APPENDIX: LIST OF VARIANTS
OF THE CINDERELLA TALE

Africa

EGYPT: Climo, Shirley. *The Egyptian Cinderella*. New York: HarperCollins Children's Books, 1989.

EGYPT: Sierra, Judy. "Rhodopis: A Cinderella in Ancient Egypt?" In *Cinderella*. The Oryx Multicultural Folktale Series. Westport, CT: Oryx, 1992.

SOUTH AFRICA: Gross, Ila Lane. "Bawa Merah." In *Cinderella Tales around the World*. New York: LEAPUSA.com, 2001.

SOUTH AFRICA: Gross, Ila Lane. "The Magic Horns." In *Cinderella Tales around the World*. New York: LEAPUSA.com, 2001.

WEST AFRICA: Onyefulu, Obi. *Chinye: A West African Folk Tale*. London: Frances Lincoln Children's Books, 1994.

ZIMBAWE: Steptoe, John. *Mufaro's Beautiful Daughters: An African Tale*. New York: Amistad, 1987.

ZULU: Phumla. *Nomi and the Magic Fish: A Story from Africa*. New York: Doubleday, 1972.

Asia

CAMBODIA: Coburn, Jewell R. *Angkat: The Cambodian Cinderella*. Arcadia, CA: Shen's Books, 1998.

CHINA: Louie, Ai-Ling. *Yeh-Shen: A Cinderella Tale from China*. New York: Penguin Putnam Books for Young Readers, 1996.

CHINA: Sierra, Judy. "Yeh-Hsien." In *Cinderella*. The Oryx Multicultural Folktale Series. Westport, CT: Oryx, 1992.

CHINA: Wilson, Barbara Ker. *Wishbones: A Folktale from China*. New York: Bradbury, 1993.

INDIA: Sierra, Judy. "How the Cowherd Found a Bride." In *Cinderella*. The Oryx Multicultural Folktale Series. Westport, CT: Oryx, 1992.

INDIA: Brucker, Meredith Babeaux. *Anklet for a Princess: A Cinderella Story from India*. Arcadia, CA: Shen's Books, 2002.

INDIA: Gross, Ila Lane. "The Black Cow." In *Cinderella Tales around the World*. New York: LEAPUSA.com, 2001.

INDIA: Mehta, Lila. *The Enchanted Anklet: a Folk Tale from India*. Cincinnati, OH: Master Communications, 1987.

INDONESIA: Gross, Ila Lane. "Red Onion, White Onion." In *Cinderella Tales around the World*. New York: LEAPUSA.com, 2001.

JAPAN: Sierra, Judy. "Benizara and Kakezara." In *Cinderella*. The Oryx Multicultural Folktale Series. Westport, CT: Oryx, 1992.

JAPAN: Schroeder, Alan. *Lily and the Wooden Bowl*. New York: Delacorte, 1994.

KOREA: Climo, Shirley. *The Korean Cinderella*. New York: HarperCollins, 1993.

LAOS: Beard, Tim, Betsy Warrick, and Kao Cho Saefong. "Old Black Snake." In *Loz-Hnoi, Loz-Hnoi Uov In the Old, Old Days*. Vol. 1 of *Traditional Stories of the Iu-Mienh*. Berkeley, CA: Laotian Handcraft Center, 1993.

MALUKU ISLANDS: Sierra, Judy. *The Gift of the Crocodile: A Cinderella Story*. New York: Simon & Schuster Books for Young Readers, 2000.

PHILIPPINES: La Paz, Myrna J. de. *Abadeha: The Philippine Cinderella*. Arcadia, CA: Shen's Books, 2001.

PHILIPPINES: Sierra, Judy. "Maria." In *Cinderella*. The Oryx Multicultural Folktale Series. Westport, CT: Oryx, 1992.

VIETNAM: Coburn, Jewell Reinhart and Tzexa Cherta Lee. *Jouanah: A Hmong Cinderella*. Arcadia, CA: Shen's Books, 1996.

VIETNAM: Lum, Darrell. *The Golden Slipper: A Vietnamese Legend*. Mahwah, NJ: Troll, 1994.

VIETNAM: Palazzo-Craig, Janet. *Tam's Slipper: A Story from Vietnam*. Mahwah, NJ: Troll, 1996.

VIETNAM: Sierra, Judy. "The Story of Tam and Cam." In *Cinderella*. The Oryx Multicultural Folktale Series. Westport, CT: Oryx, 1992.

VIETNAM: Quoc, Minh. *Tam and Cam: The Ancient Vietnamese Cinderella Story*. Manhattan Beach, CA: East West Discovery, 2006.

VIETNAM: Vuong, Lynette Dyer. "The Brocaded Slipper." In *The Brocaded Slipper and Other Vietnamese Tales*. New York: HarperCollins, 1992.

Europe

ENGLAND: Hallett, Martin and Barbara Karasek, eds. "Cap O' Rushes." In *Folk and Fairy Tales*, 4th ed. Peterborough, ON: Broadview, 2011.

ENGLAND: Haviland, Virginia. "Cap O' Rushes." In *Favorite Fairy Tales Told in England*. New York: Beech Tree Books, 1994.

ENGLAND: Jacobs, Joseph. *Tattercoats*. New York: G.P. Putnam's, 1989.

FINLAND: Sierra, Judy. "The Wonderful Birch." In *Cinderella*. The Oryx Multicultural Folktale Series. Westport, CT: Oryx, 1992.

FRANCE: Lang, Andrew, ed. "Cinderella or the Little Glass Slipper." In *The Grey Fairy Book*. Mineola, NY: Dover, 1967.

FRANCE: Perrault, Charles. "Donkey Skin." In *Tales from Perrault*. Translated by Ann Lawrence. Oxford: Oxford University Press, 1988.

FRANCE: Perrault, Charles. *Cinderella*. Translated by Anthea Bell. New York: North-South Books, 1999.

FRANCE: Perrault, Charles. "Cinderella, or the Little Glass Slipper." In *The Tales of Mother Goose*. Translated by Charles Welsh. Boston: D. C. Heath, 1901.

FRANCE: Sierra, Judy. "Cinderella, or the Little Glass Slipper." In *Cinderella*. The Oryx Multicultural Folktale Series. Westport, CT: Oryx, 1992.

GEORGIA: Sierra, Judy. "Little Rag Girl." In *Cinderella*. The Oryx Multicultural Folktale Series. Westport, CT: Oryx, 1992.

GERMANY: Grimm, Jacob and Wilhelm Grimm. "Ashenputtel." In *Grimm's Fairy Tales*. Mineola, NY: Calla, 2010.

GERMANY: Huck, Charlotte. *Princess Furball*. New York: Greenwillow Books, 1989.

GERMANY: Sierra, Judy. "Allerleirauh, or the Many-Furred Creature." In *Cinderella*. The Oryx Multicultural Folktale Series. Westport, CT: Oryx, 1992.

GERMANY: Sierra, Judy. "Little One-Eye, Little Two-Eyes, and Little Three-Eyes." In *Cinderella*. The Oryx Multicultural Folktale Series. Westport, CT: Oryx, 1992.

GREECE: Manna, Anthony and Christodoula Mitakidou. *The Orphan: A Cinderella Story from Greece*. New York: Schwartz & Wade Books, 2011.

ICELAND: Sierra, Judy. "The Story of Mjadveig, Daughter of Mani." In *Cinderella*. The Oryx Multicultural Folktale Series. Westport, CT: Oryx, 1992.

IRELAND: Climo, Shirley. *The Irish Cinderlad*. New York: HarperCollins, 1996.

IRELAND: Green, Ellin. *Billy Beg and His Bull*. New York: Holiday House, 1994.

IRELAND: DALY, Jude. *Fair, Brown & Trembling: An Irish Cinderella Story*. New York: Farrar, Straus and Giroux, 2005.

NORWAY: Lang, Andrew. "The Princess on the Glass Hill." In *The Blue Fairy Book*. Mineola, NY: Dover, 1965.

NORWAY: Haviland, Virginia. "The Princess on the Glass Hill." In *Favorite Fairy Tales Told in Norway*. New York: Beech Tree Books, 1996.

NORWAY: Sierra, Judy. "Katie Woodencloak." In *Cinderella*. The Oryx Multicultural Folktale Series. Westport, CT: Oryx, 1992.

POLAND: Jaffe, Nina. *The Way Meat Loves Salt: A Cinderella Tale from the Jewish Tradition*. New York: Henry Holt, 1998.

PORTUGAL: Sierra, Judy. "Hearth Cat." In *Cinderella*. The Oryx Multicultural Folktale Series. Westport, CT: Oryx, 1992.

RUSSIA: Mayer, Marianna. *Baba Yaga and Vasilisa the Brave*. New York: Morrow Junior Books, 1994.

RUSSIA: Haviland, Virginia. "Vasilissa the Beautiful." In *Favorite Fairy Tales Told in Russia*. New York: Beech Tree Books. 1995.

RUSSIA: Zheleznova, Irina, ed. *Vasilisa the Beautiful: Russian Fairy Tales*. Moscow: Progress, 1974.

SPAIN: Hayes, Joe. *Little Gold Star/Estrellita de oro: A Cinderella Cuento*. El Paso, TX: Cinco Puntos, 2000.

SWEDEN: Cole, Joanna, ed. "Salt and Bread." In *Best-Loved Folktales of the World*. New York: Anchor Books, 1982.

Middle East

IRAN: Climo, Shirley. *The Persian Cinderella*. New York: HarperCollins, 199.

IRAQ: Hickox, Rebecca. *The Golden Sandal: A Middle Eastern Cinderella*. New York: Holiday House, 1998.

IRAQ: Sierra, Judy. "The Little Red Fish and the Clog of Gold." In *Cinderella*. The Oryx Multicultural Folktale Series. Westport, CT: Oryx, 1992.

TURKEY: Gross, Ila Lane. "Keloglan." In *Cinderella Tales around the World*. New York: LEAPUSA.com, 2001.

North America

CANADA: Cole, Joanna, ed. "The Indian Cinderella." In *Best-Loved Folktales of the World*. New York: Anchor Books, 1982.

CARIBBEAN: San Souci, Robert D. *Cendrillon: A Caribbean Cinderella*. New York: Simon & Schuster Books for Young Readers, 1998.

HAITI: Wolkstein, Diane, comp. "The Magic Orange Tree." In *The Magic Orange Tree and Other Haitian Folktales*. New York: Knopf, 1978.

MEXICO: Coburn, Jewell Reinhart. *Domitila: A Cinderella Tale from the Mexican Tradition*. Arcadia, CA: Shen's Books, 2000.

MEXICO: DePaola, Tomie. *Adelita: A Mexican Cinderella Story*. New York: G.P. Putnam's, 2002.

USA/ALGONQUIAN: Cohlene, Terri. *Little Firefly: An Algonquian Legend*. Mahwah, NJ: Watermill Press, 1990.

USA/ALGONQUIAN: Martin, Rafe. *The Rough-Face Girl*. New York: G.P. Putnam's, 1992.

USA/APPALACHIA: Compton, Joanne. *Ashpet: An Appalachian Tale*. New York: Holiday House, 1994.

USA/APPALACHIA: Chase, Richard, ed. "Ashpet." In *Grandfather Tales: American-English Folk Tales*. New York: Houghton Mifflin, 1976.

USA/MICMAC: Sierra, Judy. "The Invisible One." In *Cinderella*. The Oryx Multicultural Folktale Series. Westport, CT: Oryx, 1992.

USA/NEW MEXICO. Hayes, Joe. "Little Gold Star." In *The Day It Snowed Tortillas: Tales from Spanish New Mexico*, 3rd ed. Santa Fe, NM: Mariposa, 1982.

USA//OJIBWA: San Souci, Robert D. *Sootface: An Ojibwa Cinderella Story*. New York: Bantam Doubleday Dell Books for Young Readers, 1994.

USA/SOUTH: Hooks, William H. *Moss Gown*. New York: Clarion Books, 1987.

USA/SOUTHWESTERN: San Souci, Robert D. *Little Gold Star: A Spanish American Cinderella Tale*. New York: HarperCollins, 2000.

USA/ZUNI: Sierra, Judy. "Poor Turkey Girl." In *Cinderella*. The Oryx Multicultural Folktale Series. Westport, CT: Oryx, 1992.

USA/ZUNI: Pollack, Penny. *The Turkey Girl: A Zuni Cinderella Story*. Boston: Little, Brown, 1996.

South America

BRAZIL: Gross, Ila Lane. "Gata Borralheira." In *Cinderella Tales around the World*. New York: LEAPUSA.com, 2001.

BRAZIL: Gross, Ila Lane. "The Maiden and the Fish." In *Cinderella Tales around the World*. New York: LEAPUSA.com, 2001.

CHILE: Gross, Ila Lane. "Maria Cinderella." In *Cinderella Tales around the World*. New York: LEAPUSA.com, 2001.

Modern

Cole, Babette. *Prince Cinders*. New York: Putnam & Gròsset, 1997.

Jackson, Ellen. *Cinder Edna*. New York: Lothrop, Lee & Shepard Books, 1994.

Kroll, Steven. *Queen of the May*. New York: Holiday House, 1993.

Lowell, Susan. *Cindy Ellen: A Wild Western Cinderella*. New York: HarperCollins, 2000.

Minters, Frances. *Cinder-Elly*. New York: Viking, 1994.

Mitchell, Marianne. *Joe Cinders*. New York: Henry Holt, 2002.

Myers, Bernice. *Sidney Rella and the Glass Sneakers*. New York, MacMillan, 1985.

Perlman, Janet. *Cinderella Penguin; or, The Little Glass Flipper*. New York: Puffin Books, 1995.

San Souci, Robert D. *Cinderella Skeleton*. San Diego: Silver Whistle, 2000.

Schroeder, Alan. *Smoky Mountain Rose: An Appalachian Cinderella*. New York: Puffin Books, 2000.

Silverman, Erica. *Raisel's Riddle*. New York: Farrar, Straus and Giroux, 1999.

Thomas, Joyce Carol. *The Gospel Cinderella*. New York: Amistad, 2004.

7

HOLIDAYS IN THE CURRICULUM

HONORING HOLIDAYS

The malls are filed with Christmas lights, Santas, and carols; the town is festooned with red-ribbon garlands on lampposts; two large Christmas trees complete with colored bulbs have just been set up in the school lobby. What about the district's non-Christian students?

There are families who have moved *from* school districts that celebrate holidays and families who have moved *to* school districts that celebrate the holidays. In some districts there is controversy on the subject of holiday celebration within the classroom. Some holidays celebrated are secular, such as Thanksgiving and Veterans Day; some, such as Halloween, are based on religious traditions; and some are actual religious celebrations.

It is primarily the Christian holidays, such as Christmas, that are celebrated in many of our schools. However, religious and ethnic diversity is growing in our schools. A few of our students do not observe holidays at all.

Celebrations and holiday traditions are part of our cultures. It is can be a cheerless school that contains no decorations when the world outside the classroom is festooned with lights or candles or pumpkins. Some of our students cannot afford to have trimmings in their homes, and school may be the sole opportunity for participation in decorative traditions.

It is important to become aware of *all* our students' cultures—the current students and people whom they might meet. Classes should not *celebrate* the holidays, but they can study them as multicultural inquiries. This is quite different from decorating a room with Christmas trees and lights and then asking the one Jewish child to "tell us about *your* holiday" or "bring in *your* menorah."

When the teacher discusses Christmas, Hanukkah, and Kwanzaa as examples of festivals celebrated by different cultures and students then research unfamiliar holidays, decorating the room and reading and writing books, making PowerPoint presentations, creating puppet shows, performing skits, or otherwise sharing their research, everyone is valued. In many instances, students actually can learn more about the holidays they celebrate at home. Just imagine a room with colorful decorations from all cultures!

There would not be much purpose in studying the same holidays each year of school. However, schools could divide the holidays by grade level. One grade level could investigate winter holidays, one the spring and summer celebrations, and one the fall festivities, whether secular or religious.

There are many winter holidays that are celebrated around the time of Christmas. For example:

- *Bodhi Day (Rohatsu)* is celebrated by Buddhists on December 8.
- *Boxing Day* (Australian, Canadian, English, Irish) is December 26.
- *Chanukah (Hanukkah)* is the Jewish Festival of Lights; the eight-day celebration is based on the Jewish calendar and it is celebrated sometime within late November or December.
- *Chinese New Year* is celebrated at the end of January or, beginning of February, six weeks after the winter solstice.
- *Christmas* is celebrated most commonly on December 25 by different Christian traditions and celebrations in different sects and divergent cultures.
- *Diwali* is the Hindu Festivals of Lights and falls on October or November on a new moon day.
- *Dongzhi* is celebrated in China on the winter solstice (December 21–23) to celebrate the winter harvest.
- *Las Posadas* is a Mexican celebration celebrated for nine days, beginning December 16.

- *Lohri* is a harvest festival celebrated in northern India on January 13.
- *Los Reyes (Three Kings' Day)* is celebrated in Hispanic and Latin cultures, such as Puerto Rico, Spain, and Mexico, on January 6; this holiday is celebrated as *Epiphany* by Western Christian cultures.
- *Midwinter Ceremony* is celebrated by the Iroquois in January or February, depending on the moon cycle.
- *Ōmisoka* is celebrated in Japan on December 31, the last day of the year.
- *Ramadan*, an Islamic religious observance, is part of a lunar-based calendar and, therefore, is celebrated at different times in different years. In certain years only, it occurs around the time of Christmas.
- *Saint Nicholas Day* is celebrated on December 6 in many European countries and in America in many European communities.
- *Shab-e Yaldâ (Shab-e Chelleh)* is celebrated on the eve of the winter solstice (December 20–21) in Iran by followers of many religions. It originated in Zoroastrianism, the state religion that preceded Islam.
- *Soyaluna* is the Hopi winter solstice festival celebrated on December 22.
- *Winter Solstice* is a holiday increasingly observed by many worldwide.

The winter-holiday study could begin in November with Thanksgiving and continue through February (Valentine's Day). Rooms can be decorated with artifacts—both authentic and student-manufactured—and posters and decorations created by the students who would share their research in some distinctive manner.

As an alternative, the design of holiday study could be based on the school district's social studies curriculum—students in the three grades could research holidays by the time period or geographical location they are learning about in their social studies unit.

For those studying ancient cultures, there are celebrations such as the winter solstice celebrations of ancient Brazil and Egypt. In ancient Greece, the winter solstice ritual was called Lenaia, the Festival of the Wild Women, while in ancient Rome, Saturnalia was celebrated. Kwanzaa is a relatively modern African-American holiday, created by 1966 by Doctor Maulana Karenga. In some states, students study world cultures in sixth and seventh grades; the study of holidays would complement those units.

The examination of cultural holidays easily lends itself surprisingly well to interdisciplinary units:

- Social Studies: The social studies curriculum could serve as a catalyst for whatever time period or culture is being covered.

- Science: Many holidays have a scientific basis. The winter solstice celebrations and the harvest festivals have their foundations in the laws of nature, and research would investigate those connections. Determining which winter solstice celebrations are in December and which are in June leads to a study of hemispheric seasons. A class researching Hanukkah could experiment lighting with oil, trying to determine the amount of oil necessary for a time length of light.

- Mathematics: Since many holidays are dependent on a lunar calendar or a system other than our Julian calendar, mathematicians need to determine the yearly date of holidays such as Ramadan and the date of the Chinese New Year depending on the winter solstice date. Some of the celebrations employ quite complicated mathematical calculations.

- Language Arts: Students read holiday stories or read tales associated with the traditions of the culture or holidays itself or write a journal of their findings or their own holiday stories. Another venture is a collaborative class compilation of a *Holidays for Dummies* text.

- Art: Artists create appropriate decorations and sculpture fitting artifacts.

- Home Economics: Students can prepare traditional foods and study serving ceremonies.

- Physical Education and Music: Many holidays have traditional games, music, and dances for classes to pursue or for students to individually research and attempt during these class periods.

Each student may be assigned to take responsibility for a holiday at some point during the year, either individually or as part of a collaborative group. The research could be presented either at the time of the holiday or during one Respect for Holidays Week, a prime choice being prior to winter break when the rooms would look as festive as, although distinct from, the outside world.

After researching the holidays of all cultures, students could fashion their own unique, secular, local celebration such as the "Festivus" holiday created by the writers for the television show *Seinfeld*.

THE HOLIDAY SPIRIT OF GIVING

Most holidays involve some sort of gift-giving or expression of gratitude or sacrifice on behalf of the community or others. Therefore, a divergent way to pay heed to the holidays or holiday seasons is to use them as occasions to help or give to others.

One grade-level team of homerooms traditionally "celebrates" the winter holidays by making candy-cane reindeer that students then deliver to a local nursing home. They take a one- or two-hour break from classes on a day prior to the holidays, and the students each make a reindeer by gluing on eyes and a puff-ball nose, twisting pipe cleaners into antlers, and tying a bow and gift card around the "neck" of the candy cane.

Sitting in groups, the students chat and work collaboratively. Some groups generally organize an assembly line, distributing the supplies, working the glue gun, tying the bows, and so forth.

The week before the "reindeer" are taken to the senior citizens, they serve as decorations and enliven the classroom, giving it a holiday look. If reindeer are too Christmasy, candy canes now are available in a range of colors and flavors, and alternate "animals" or gifts can be made from them. These presents can be taken to nursing homes and children's hospitals, or given in gratitude from the team to school personnel such as secretaries, maintenance workers, and cafeteria staff.

In classes students can create gifts for other children, those in hospitals or shelters, or to be sent to economically disadvantaged areas. In academic classes, students can write books, either fiction or nonfiction. An inexpensive way to make lasting hardcover books is to purchase "Bare Books" (www.barebooks.com) and write and illustrate directly on the page or insert pages with double-sided tape. Costing less than two dollars per book, the money could be donated or raised if funds are not available. The authors employ the information gained about writing or content area curriculum to write the books, which makes it a win-win situation—both academic and community service.

On other occasions students have created and sent holiday cards. For Thanksgiving or Valentine's Day, appreciation cards can be sent to servicemen or to staff members or members of the community. On Father's and Mother's Day, students wrote poems and each created a card for a man or woman who has been important in a student's life. Composing the text and making the actual cards is an effective use of technology, as students play with layout and fonts and drawing programs.

The cards are neat, professional, legible, and free. For those students who cannot go to a store or do not have the money for cards or presents, this activity lets them give something memorable to family members.

A class or groups of students can also substitute gift-giving by raising money for a charity. Student groups have baked and sold cookies to raise money and then sought charities, such as Oprah's Angels, that do not take a percentage of the donation for administrative costs and also offer a choice of beneficiaries interesting to adolescents.

Combining celebrations with community service, students can commemorate the harvest holidays by planting or tending gardens on school grounds or in their community.

There are many ways that holidays and the spirit of celebration can be acknowledged in a nondenominational and secular fashion.

ACADEMIC HOLIDAY CELEBRATIONS

At times it is part of the school culture to celebrate holidays that may be perceived as secular occasions. Some school calendars actually schedule times for team or school-wide activities. This commonly occurs in some schools at Halloween, but some students do not observe this holiday. Therefore, instead of celebrating the holiday, teachers can invite students to wear "costumes" and bring in appropriate treats as part of a content unit.

Students can disguise themselves as characters in literature or history, as vocabulary words, as planets or ecosystems, or as geometric shapes or part of a fraction. Treats can also fit into time periods, places, and environments, be cut into geometric shapes, be decorated, or serve as fractions. One student made plum duff to augment a reading of a tall tale in which the dessert was featured.

In this way, celebrations can be turned into festivals of learning.

APPENDIX: MULTICULTURAL HOLIDAY PICTURE BOOKS

Aminah, Ibrahim Ali. *The Three Muslim Festivals*. Skokie, IL: IQRA' International Educational Foundation, 1998.

Angell, Carole S. *Celebrations around the World: A Multicultural Handbook*. Golden, CO: Fulcrum, 1996.

Conrad, Heather. *Lights of Winter: Winter Celebrations around the World*. New York: Lightport Books, 2001.

Elya, Susan Middleton and Merry Banks. *N Is for Navidad*. San Francisco: Chronicle Books, 2007.

Jackson, Ellen. *The Winter Solstice*. Brookfield, CT: Millbrook 1997.

Jones, Lynda. *Kids around the World Celebrate! The Best Feasts and Festivals from Many Lands*. New York: John Wiley, 2000.

Luenn, Nanacy. *Celebrations of Light: A Year of Holidays around the World*. New York: Atheneum Books for Young Readers, 1998.

Pfeffer, Wendy. *The Shortest Day: Celebrating the Winter Solstice*. New York: Dutton Children's Books, 2003.

Reynolds, Betty. *Japanese Celebrations: Cherry Blossoms, Lanterns and Stars!* North Claredon, VT: Turtle, 2006.

Tabor, Nany María Grande. *Celebrations: Holidays of the United States of America and Mexico*. Watertown, MA: Charlesbridge, 2004.

Additional resources are available at http://cutureforkids.com.

8

READING FOR RESPECT

They sit in small groups scattered around the classroom, deep in discussion. In one group, Sarah is reading *Max the Mighty* (Philbrick 1998); John, *Whale Talk* (Crutcher 2001); Jen, *Fade to Black* (Flinn 2005); and Tom and Dave are partner-reading *The Bully* (Langan 2002). Their discussion centers on the central issue of bullying and how it is portrayed in each of their novels and how each of their characters handles bullying. Over the next few weeks, as the book club members get deeper into their books and become more comfortable with each other, the talk shifts to personal experiences, as victim or witness to bullying or as bully. After they finish reading and discussing their books, the group will go to the library to conduct research and together plan a presentation to their class.

Another group is reading books on body image, novels such as *Perfect* (Friend, 2004), *Wintergirls* (Anderson 2009), *One Fat Summer* (Lipsyte 1991), the memoirs *'Til the Fat Girl Sings* (Wheatley 2006), and *Stick Figure* (Gottlieb 2001). The members of the book club will research anorexia, bulimia, and weight loss fads and are debating whether to create a poster of graphs and charts for the gym hallway or a warning brochure for teens.

A third book club reads novels that center on the topic of building relationships, while the fourth group is reading a variety of nonfiction self-help books geared toward developing self-respect.

In all book clubs, each of the readers is reading a different text at a different reading level, exemplifying a discrete aspect of an issue.

Language arts class? Maybe. But this could as easily be a health class. And in a social studies class, some groups could be reading books dealing with multicultural issues of contemporary teens while others read about characters who dealt with discrimination in different time periods.

There are many ways for teachers to use literature in the classroom to facilitate building respect both for other students and for other peoples and to help their students acquire self-respect. Stories give readers different perspectives and can place them in positions and situations in which they have never been; stories let the readers take part in experiences outside their realms.

Literature can put the readers in the role of the *other* and allow them to experience life from the *other* side. Stories help readers make sense of themselves and their worlds. Through stories, readers can define relationships and vicariously view those that work and analyze why and how they work. Readers can also consider unique ways to handle problems and find creative solutions.

Fictional stories explore "what ifs" and have more flexibility in depiction of characters, plots, and events, while creative nonfiction portrays authentic events, real people, and/or actual conflicts. This genre, which has been becoming more popular, allows readers to see paths taken, goals achieved, victories won—historically and by their contemporaries.

Nonfiction books and articles that emphasize issues of relationships, bullying, self-image, and cultural clashes and conflicts of all kinds and provide information about the beliefs, traditions, and customs of diverse cultures are extremely valuable, and reading this genre gives students more experience reading nonfiction texts, rather than textbooks.

While much of this reading lends itself to the language arts class, it is imperative that students read across the curriculum in all content areas. Many of the reading resources in this chapter lend themselves to other content area readings and discussions.

READING DIFFERENT TYPES OF TEXT

The teacher stands in front of the classroom, reading aloud with inflection and expression. The students sit, rapt with attention. This could be an elementary, middle, or high school class in any content area. The teacher could be reading a news article, a poem, a picture book, an excerpt from a novel or nonfiction book, or any text at all.

Picture Books

Picture books are a primary way to include read-alouds in all grade levels. It has been proven advantageous for teachers to read aloud across the curriculum, at all grade levels. Reading aloud to children helps them develop and improve their literacy skills: reading, writing, speaking, vocabulary development, and especially listening. Read-alouds allow for teachers to think aloud—modeling what they are thinking, what comprehension and thinking strategies they are using—and give examples of critical thinking: analysis, synthesis, and evaluation. Read-alouds also generate whole-class discussion and provide a shared experience.

Picture books have the added advantage of incorporating illustrations that enhance meaning and perspective. Multicultural picture books include illustrations that bring other cultures—past and present—alive, as long as they are accurately represented. Here is where teachers need to check their resources and explain the differences between cultural, historical, and contemporary life.

Short Stories, Essays, and Articles

Not all teachers have the luxury of including book-length texts in their curriculum; therefore, short stories and essay collections are time-saving glimpses into an issue, a culture, or another time period. Short stories also can serve as an introduction to an issue or genre study in which longer texts will be read. Many teachers have found that including short stories about specific historic time periods, such as that of the Holocaust, serve to quickly take their students back in time; and contemporary short stories of other cultures help readers to understand a range of perspectives.

Short story or essay collections based around a theme permit students to explore issues from multiple sides and angles. For example, the stories from *Prejudice* (Muse 1995) illustrate the facing prejudice from a wide range of experiences: prejudice based on race, religion, body image, socioeconomic status, physical disability, and culture. Informational articles from journals, magazines, and newspapers can supplement the health, science, and math curricula.

Poetry

When poetry is infused into the curriculum, the mystery of the genre is removed; students become more comfortable with poetry (which is appearing more frequently on standardized and Advanced Placement tests), and poems allow readers to experience the life of *others* more intimately than through other texts. Poetry also lends itself to read-alouds, either by the teacher or the students as they *become* the narrator and decide *how* the poem is to be read (see chapter 3). Individual poems such as "Myself" by Edgar Guest can also be used to open discussions—in this case, on self-respect—to introduce issue studies.

READING IN DIVERSE WAYS

Whole-Class Shared Reading

One means to employ literature in the classroom to study diversity, culture, and issues of respect is to read a whole-class, shared text and study and discuss the issues together. A method to connect the reader and the character in a fictional text or the narrator in a memoir or creative nonfiction is through some of the activities described earlier in the book. Readers can write an "I Am" poem as the character or narrator of a text or create a poem in two voices between the reader and a character, as in "Teenagers" (chapter 2).

Mary wrote a poem in two voices, comparing herself to Anne Frank, a girl with a different religion who lived long time ago and under greatly dissimilar conditions. Afteward she reflected, "Despite differences in time or appearance, people can be similar to each other. We may be different in many ways, but we are similar too. We all have emotions and personalities and, despite color and creed, we all connect in different ways. Sometimes prejudice gets in the way of that" (Roessing 2005, 9). Mary can extend those same reflections when comparing herself to classmates and other people in her current world.

Small-Group Collaborative Reading: Book Clubs

An even more effective way to read and share this type of literature is through book clubs, also known as literature circles. When implementing book clubs, the teacher can select literature with a variety of cultural or alienation issues in a range of reading levels, differentiating so that all students can participate.

The entire class can focus on one issue with each book club reading a different text. For example, if the class were focusing on the issue of alienation, or not fitting in, the five book clubs could read different novels:

- *The Chocolate War* (Cormier 1974)
- *Speak* (Anderson 2006)
- *The Misfits* (Howe 2001)
- *Dairy Queen* (Murdock 2006)
- *Freak the Mighty* (Philbrick 1993)

If a class were to examine different cultural issues, either contemporary or historical, the teacher would chose five different books in sets of five or six and students would then choose issues and books based on their interests and reading level, and form five groups:

- Self-respect: *We Beat the Streets* (Davis, Jenkins, and Hunt 2005)
- Acceptance and respect: *Define Normal* (Peters 2000)
- Multicultural issues: *Esperanza Rising* (Ryan 2000)
- Bullying: *The Skin I'm In* (Flake 1998)
- Body image: *Boost* (Mackel 2008)

In a third scenario, the class would investigate a range of issues; members of each book club would read a different book, some fiction, some nonfiction, on the issue as illustrated at the beginning of this chapter.

Before choosing books and, thus, clubs, it is advantageous for the teacher to book-talk each selection so that students have advanced notice of the topic and issues in each book. The students then browse the books, noting the author's writing style and reading level of the text, and list their two top choices. The teacher can then build the groups with appropriate students and texts while still allowing for choice.

Each group reads its book according to a schedule cooperatively planned by the members. Book clubs meet at a scheduled time during class, possibly fifteen to twenty minutes twice a week or every other day, and discuss the issues in the book, the problems and conflicts generated by these issues, and the way the characters handled these obstacles. The strength of book clubs is that students direct the discussions. When students respond to their daily reading using a two sided-double entry form, they bring their thoughts to each meeting to discuss (figures 8.1, 8.2, 8.3). "Written responses assist the shy members and forgetful students in contributing to the conversation . . . Another benefit is that journaling provides a record for revisiting a past discussion point" (Roessing 2009, 83).

On this journal, members summarize what they have read—and list what they know, want or need to know—and learned about the issues portrayed in the book. On the back of the journal page, readers can track the problems the characters or narrators (in the case of nonfiction) encounter and, on the left side of the sheet, how they deal with those problems. On the right side, readers reflects on their own responses; on personal, other text, or real-world connections; on inferences and predictions; and on feelings or research.

Following are a sample front page of a book club response form and samples of two second page forms, the first (figure 8.2) to be used when reading the beginning of a book, as the characters and conflicts are introduced, and the second (figure 8.3) to be used further into the book, as the characters begin attempting to solve their problems.

During or after reading, each book club should conduct research to supplement the facts and ideas disclosed by their reading, their books providing topics and questions to effect an inquiry. Book club members would then prepare a presentation for the class.

If time is an issue, article clubs or short story clubs can be substituted; however, more empathy is achieved when readers "live" the life of the *other* through developed characters going through conflicts, testing diverse solutions. Articles tend to present issues and identify the problems and solutions, and short stories are, necessarily, less developed.

Name _____ Title _____ Chapters ____ to ____

The ISSUE in this book is _____ (bullying, body image, etc)

What I KNOW about this issue	What I WANT/NEED to know	What I LEARNED or FOUND OUT

SUMMARY of what happens in these chapters:

_____

_____

_____

_____

_____

_____

_____

_____

_____

_____

_____

Figure 8.1. Front Side of Book Club Response Journal

Name _____ Title _____ Chapters ____to ____

WHAT HAPPENS IN THE BOOK	WHAT I AM THINKING ABOUT THAT
The main characters' TRAITS: physical and personality	
Character:	
Character:	
Some of the PROBLEMS the characters face	
Some of the CAUSES of the problems	

Figure 8.2. Back Side of Book Club Response Journal—use for first half of the novel

WHAT HAPPENS IN THE BOOK	WHAT I AM THINKING ABOUT THAT
Some of the PROBLEMS/ISSUES the characters face	
Some of the CAUSES of the problems	
Ways the characters DEAL with these problems	

Name _____ Title _____ Chapters ____ to ____

Figure 8.3. Back Side of Book Club Response Journal—use for second half of the novel

Individual Self-Selected Reading

Although young adolescent students enjoy working in book clubs because they are supportive and social, it is also effective for students to read self-selected texts when possible. Usually students are more motivated to read texts that they choose and in which they are interested; this makes for a student-centered classroom. Again, books can center around one issue or a variety of issues that all relate to respect. The Reading Resources list at the end of the chapter lists a variety of texts of different issues, reading genres, reading lengths, and reading and interest levels, fiction and nonfiction.

READING ACROSS THE CURRICULUM

In social studies, novels about disenfranchised groups or challenges faced by diverse cultural groups—by ethnicity, race, gender, geography, age, socioeconomic status—appropriate to issues of the time period of the curriculum, could be read, while in health class curriculum issues, such as bullying, body image, teamwork, gender roles, and self-respect, could be examined.

FREE WRITING FOR FOCUSED DISCUSSION

Another approach to employ texts in classes across the curriculum is to utilize texts as prompts for free writing. Free writing is an effective way to induce students to begin thinking about a topic or issue and to write about it, leading to more in-depth and critical class discussions. The very "freeness" of free writing encourages and supports the most reluctant writers to write. When students have tangible ideas on the paper or journal in front of them, they are more likely to contribute to the conversation.

Free writing is writing anything that the writers think of in response to a prompt. In many cases, writers are invited to either write directly on the subject of the prompt or write on any topic that the prompt makes them consider. What is so liberating about this format is that writers may write in any format—story, memoir, poem, letter, stream of consciousness, list, essay, fiction, nonfiction, humorous, serious, in the perspective of first person or third person, and so forth.

There is only one free writing rule—writers need to write for the entire time. A good length is approximately eight minutes, depending on how comfortable the class is with free writing and the length of the class period and, most importantly, on the allowance of adequate time for sharing. There are no other rules in free writing, except to write the entire time. Writers are not to worry about spelling, grammar, or punctuation as long as the writing communicates. Free writing can also be used as brainstorming for future developed writings.

Teachers can read excerpts from books, poetry, magazines, news articles and headlines, quotations, or songs, and use music and artwork as free writing prompts. Many of the following resources can be used as prompts that will lead to discussions, either to introduce a unit or within a unit. Historical texts can be employed to introduce conversations on contemporary issues, such as immigration, and current texts can be used to introduce historical events, especially events that center on intolerance and acceptance.

APPENDIX: READING RESOURCES

Following is a list of literature and other helpful resources that emphasize the issues and topics discussed in this book—tolerance, alienation, fitting in, bullying, acceptance, body image, self-respect, multiculturalism, building community, and respecting diversity. These books would be beneficial additions to any classroom library, for common reads and discussions, for free writing activities, or, in the case of picture books and poetry, to introduce issue focus lessons and to begin classroom conversations and discussions on these important topics.

Books are marked by topics, most frequently *bullying, body image, alienation* (not fitting in or feeling "different"), *cultural conflicts, gender issues, contemporary immigration, multiculturalism, diversity, acceptance, self-respect,* or *respect,* although many topics overlap, as a recent immigrant may feel alienated because of issues of culture or GLBTQ teens may be bullied by their peers.

Picture Books

Bateman, Teresa. *The Bully Blockers Club*. Morton Grove, IL: Albert Whitman, 2004. [bullying]

Buckley, Carol. *Tarra & Bella: The Elephant and Dog Who Became Best Friends*. New York, G.P. Putnam's, 2009. [acceptance]

Bunting, Eve. *A Picnic in October*. San Diego: Harcourt Brace, 1999. [contemporary immigration]

Bunting, Eve. *One Green Apple*. New York: Clarion Books, 2006. [alienation; contemporary immigration]

Cannon, Janel. *Stellaluna*. New York: Scholastic, 1993. [acceptance]

Capone, Deb. *Dumplings are Delicious*. Montauk, NY: As Simple As That, 2005. [multiculturalism]

Caseley, Judith. *Bully*. New York: Greenwillow Books, 2001. [bullying]

Cole, Babette. *Princess Smartypants*. New York: G.P. Putnam's 1991. [self-respect]

Couric, Katie. *The Brand New Kid*. New York: Doubleday, 2000. [bullying; acceptance]

DePaola, Tomie. *Oliver Button is a Sissy*. San Diego: Voyager Books, 1979. [acceptance; gender roles]

Dooley, Norah. *Everybody Bakes Bread*. Minneapolis, MN: Carolrhoda Books, 1996. [multiculturalism]

Dooley, Norah. *Everybody Brings Noodles*. Minneapolis, MN: Carolrhoda Books, 2002. [multiculturalism]

Dooley, Norah. *Everybody Cooks Rice*. Minneapolis, MN: Carolrhoda Books, 1991. [multiculturalism]

Dooley, Norah. *Everybody Serves Soup*. Minneapolis, MN: Carolrhoda Books, 2000. [multiculturalism]

Fox, Mem. *Feathers and Fools*. San Diego: Voyager Books, 1989. [acceptance]

Fox, Mem. *Whoever You Are*. San Diego: Voyager Books, 2001. [multiculturalism; acceptance]

Golenbock, Peter. *Teammates*. San Diego: Voyager Books, 1990. [acceptance]

Grossman, Linda Sky. *Respect is Correct*. Toronto, ON: Second Story, 2002. [respect]

Hoffman, Mary. *Amazing Grace*. New York: Dial Books for Young Readers, 1991. [self-respect; acceptance]

Hoffman, Mary. *The Color of Home*. New York: Phyllis Fogelman Books, 2002. [contemporary immigration]

Howe, James. *I Wish I Were a Butterfly*. New York: Harcourt Children's Books, 1987. [self-respect]

Isadora, Rachel. *Max*. New York: Aladdin, 1976. [acceptance; gender roles]

Knight, Margy Burns. *Who Belongs Here? An American Story*. Gardiner, ME: Tilbury House 1993. [acceptance; contemporary immigration]

Ludwig, Trudy. *Just Kidding*. Berkeley, CA: Tricycle, 2006. [bullying]

Ludwig, Trudy. *My Secret Bully*. Berkeley, CA: Tricycle, 2004. [bullying]

Ludwig, Trudy. *Too Perfect*. Berkeley, CA: Tricycle, 2009. [self-respect]

Ludwig, Trudy. *Trouble Talk*. Berkeley, CA: Tricycle, 2008. [bullying]

McCain, Becky Ray. *Nobody Knew What to Do: A Story About Bullying*. Morton Grove, IL: Albert Whitman, 2001. [bullying]

Moss, Peggy. *One of Us*. Gardiner, ME: Tilbury House, 2010. [acceptance; diversity]

Moss, Peggy. *Say Something*. Gardiner, ME: Tilbury House, 2008. [bullying]

Myers, Walter Dean. *Looking Like Me*. New York: Egmont USA, 2009. [self-respect]

Nikola-Lisa, W. *Bein' with You This Way*. New York: Lee & Low Books, 1994. [diversity]

Parr, Todd. *It's Okay to Be Different*. New York: Little, Brown Books for Young Readers, 2009. [diversity; self-respect]

Parton, Dolly. *Coat of Many Colors*. New York: HarperCollins, 1994. [self-respect; SES]

Perry, Marie Fritz. *A Gift for Sadia*. Northfield, MN: Buttonweed, 2005. [contemporary immigration]

Schreck, Karen Halvorsen. *Lucy's Family Tree*. Gardiner, ME: Tilbury House, 2006. [diversity; self-acceptance]

Whitcomb, Mary E. *Odd Velvet*. San Francisco: Chronicle Books, 1998. [acceptance; self-esteem]

Yang, Belle. *Hannah Is My Name: A Young Immigrant's Story*. Cambridge, MA: Candlewick, 2007. [contemporary immigration]

Zolotow, Charlotte. *William's Doll*. New York: HarperCollins, 1985. [acceptance; gender roles]

Short Story, Essay, and Poetry Collections

Bauer, Marion Dane, ed. *Am I Blue? Coming Out from the Silence*. New York: HarperCollins, 1995.

Carlson, Lori M., ed. *American Eyes: New Asian-American Short Stories for Young Adults*. New York: Fawcett Juniper, 1994.

Carlson, Lori M., ed. *Cool Salsa: Bilingual Poems on Growing Up Latino in the United States*. With an introduction by Oscar Hijuelos. New York: Henry Holt, 1994.

Erno, Jeff. *Bullied*. Frisco, TX: Dreamspinner, 2011.

Feelings, Tom, ed. *Soul Looks Back In Wonder*. New York: Dial Books, 1993.

Franco, Betsy, ed. *Things I Have to Tell You: Poems and Writings by Teenage Girls*. Cambridge, MA: Candlewick, 2001.

Franco, Betsy, ed. *You Hear Me? Poems and Writings by Teenage Boys*. Cambridge, MA: Candlewick, 2001.

Frosch, Mary, ed. *Coming of Age in America: A Multicultural Anthology*. With an introduction by Gary Soto. New York: New Press, 2007.

Gallo, Donald R., ed. *First Crossing: Stories about Teen Immigrants*. Cambridge, MA: Candlewick, 2004.

Gallo, Donald R., ed. *Join In: Multiethnic Short Stories*. New York: Bantam Doubleday Dell Books for Young Readers, 1993.

Gallo, Donald R., ed. *No Easy Answers: Short Stories about Teenagers Making Tough Choices*. New York: Bantam Doubleday Dell Books for Young Readers, 1997.

Gallo, Donald R., ed. *On the Fringe*. New York: Dial Books, 2001.

Howe, James, ed. *13: Thirteen Stories That Capture the Agony and Ecstasy of Being Thirteen*. New York: Atheneum, 2003.

Humphrey, Sandra McLeod. *Hot Issues, Cool Choices: Facing Bullies, Peer Pressure, Popularity, and Put-Downs*. Amherst, New York: Prometheus Books, 2007.

Khan, Rukhsana. *Muslim Child: Understanding Islam through Stories and Poems*. Morton Grove, IL: Albert Whitman, 2002.

Mazer, Anne, ed. *America Street: A Multicultural Anthology of Stories*. New York: Persea Books, 1993.

Mazer, Anne, ed. *Going Where I'm Coming From: Memoirs of American Youth*. New York: Persea Books, 1995.

Muse, Daphne, ed. *Prejudice: Stories about Hate, Ignorance, Revelation, and Transformation*. New York: Hyperion, 1995.

Ortiz Cofer, Judith. *An Island Like You: Stories of the Barrio*. New York: Orchard Books, 1995.

Singer, Bennett L., ed. *Growing Up Gay/Lesbian: A Literary Anthology*. New York: New Press, 1994.

Stavans, Ilan. *Wachale!: Poetry and Prose about Growing Up Latino*. Peterborough, NH: Cricket Books/Marcato, 2001.

Novels

Alexie, Sherman. *The Absolutely True Diary of a Part-Time Indian*. New York: Little, Brown, 2007. [alienation; multiculturalism]

Anderson, Lauri Halse. *Speak*. New York: Speak, 2009. [alienation; rape]

Anderson, Lauri Halse. *Wintergirls*. New York: Viking, 2009. [body image]

Atkins, Catherine. *Alt Ed.* New York: Speak, 2003. [bullying, body image, respect]

Barcellona, Kelley Powell. *The Hive.* New York: Pegasus Books for Children, 2009. [bullying]

Cisneros, Sandra. *The House on Mango Street.* New York: Vintage Books, 1991. [multiculturalism]

Ortiz Cofer, Judith. *Call Me Maria.* New York: Scholastic, 2004. [contemporary immigration]

Crew, Linda. *Children of the River.* New York: Bantam Doubleday Dell Books for Young Readers, 1989. [contemporary immigration; multicultural]

Cromier, Robert. *The Chocolate War.* New York: Dell Laurel-Leaf, 1974. [alienation]

Crutcher, Chris. *Whale Talk.* New York: HarperTeen, 2009. [alienation, respect]

Crutcher, Chris. *Staying Fat for Sarah Byrnes.* New York: HarperTempest, 2003. [alienation]

Flake, Sharon G. *The Skin I'm In.* New York: Hyperion Books for Children, 1998. [bullying; self-respect]

Fleischman, Paul. *Seedfolks.* New York: HaperCollins, 1997. [community-building]

Flinn, Alex. *Fade to Black.* New York: HarperTempest, 2005. [bullying; HIV]

Friend, Natasha. *Perfect: A Novel.* Minneapolis, MN: Milkweed 2004. [body image]

Frost, Helen. *Keesha's House.* New York: Farrar, Straus and Giroux, 2003. [alienation]

Garden, Nancy. *Annie on My Mind.* New York: Farrar, Straus and Giroux, 2007. [alienation; sexual orientation]

Haddon, Mark. *The Curious Incident of the Dog in the Night-Time.* New York: Vintage Books, 2003. [alienation-special needs]

Hartinger, Brent. *Geography Club.* New York: HarperTempest, 2004. [alienation; sexual orientation]

Hautzig, Deborah. *Second Star to the Right.* New York: Puffin Books, 1999. [body image]

Holland, Isabelle. *Heads You Win, Tails I Lose.* New York: Fawcett Juniper, 1973. [body image]

Howe, James. *The Misfits.* New York: Aladdin, 2001. [alienation]

Howe, James. *Totally Joe.* New York: Atheneum Books for Young Readers, 2005. [alienation; sexual orientation]

Korman, Gordon. *Schooled.* New York: Hyperion Paperbacks for Children, 2007. [bullying]

Levenkron, Steven. *The Best Little Girl in the World.* New York: Warner Books, 1997. [body image]

Langan, Paul. *The Bully*. Bluford Series. West Berlin, NJ: Townsend, 2002. [bullying]

Lipsyte, Robert. *One Fat Summer*. New York: HarperCollins, 1991. [body image]

Ludwig, Trudy. *Confessions of a Former Bully*. Berkeley, CA: Tricycle Press, 2010. [bullying]

Mackler, Carolyn. *The Earth, My Butt, and Other Big Round Things*. Cambridge, MA: Candlewick, 2003. [body image]

Mancusi, Mari. *Gamer Girl*. New York: Dutton Children's Books. 2008. [alienation]

Mazer, Norma Fox. *Mrs. Fish, Ape, and Me, the Dump Queen*. New York: Dutton, 1980. [alienation; relationships]

Menzie, Morgan. *Diary of an Anorexic Girl*. Nashville, TN: W Publishing, 2003. [body image]

Miklowitz, Gloria. *The War Between the Classes*. New York: Dell Laurel-Leaf, 1986. [acceptance; diversity; class]

Mackel, Kathy. *Boost*. New York: Dial Books, 2008. [body image; steroid use]

Murdock, Catherine Gilbert. *Dairy Queen*. New York: Graphia, 2006. [alienation]

Newman, Lesléa. *Fat Chance*. New York: Putnam & Grosset Group, 1996. [body image]

Nye, Naomi Shihab. *Habibi*. New York: Aladdin, 1999. [cultural conflict]

Oates, Joyce Carol. *Big Mouth & Ugly Girl*. New York: HarperTempest, 2002. [alienation; relationships]

Pearsall, Shelley. *All of the Above*. New York: Little, Brown, 2006. [alienation]

Perkins, Mitali. *The Not-So-Star-Spangled Life of Sunita Sen*. New York: Little, Brown, 2005. [relationships; cultural conflict]

Peters, Julie Anne. *Define "Normal."* Boston, MA: Little, Brown, 2000. [respect for differences]

Peters, Julie Anne. *Keeping You a Secret*. New York: Little, Brown Books for Young Readers, 2005. [intolerance; self-respect; sexual orientation]

Peters, Julie Anne. *Luna*. New York: Little, Brown, 2004. [alienation; sexual orientation]

Philbrick, Rodman. *Freak the Mighty*. New York: Scholastic, 1993. [alienation]

Philbrick, Rodman. *Max the Mighty*. New York: Scholastic, 1998. [bullying]

Picoult, Jodi. *Nineteen Minutes*. New York: Washington Square, 2008. [bullying]

Ryan, Pam Muñoz. *Esperanza Rising*. New York: Scholastic, 2001. [cultural conflict]

Sitomer, Alan Lawrence. *The Secret Story of Sonia Rodriquez*. New York: Hyperion, 2008. [cultural conflicts]

Sonnenblick, Jordan. *Notes from the Midnight Driver.* New York: Scholastic, 2006. [respect for elders]

Soto, Gary. *Jesse.* New York: Harcourt Brace, 1994. [cultural conflicts; socio-economic status]

Spinelli, Jerry. *Crash.* New York: Alfred A. Knopf, 1996. [bullying]

Spinelli, Jerry. *Maniac Magee.* New York: Little, Brown, 1990. [tolerance]

Spinelli, Jerry. *Stargirl.* New York: Alfred A. Knopf, 2000. [alienation; acceptance of differences]

Stren, Patti. *I Was a 15-Year-Old Blimp.* New York: Harper and Row, 1985. [body image]

Voigh, Cynthia. *Izzy, Willy-Nilly.* New York: Atheneum Books for Young Readers, 2005. [alienation]

Wieler, Diana. *Bad Boys.* Toronto, ON: Groundwood Books, 2010. [alienation; tolerance]

Wilhelm, Doug. *The Revealers.* New York: Farrar, Straus and Giroux, 2003. [bullying]

Wittingler, Ellen. *Parrotfish.* New York: Simon & Schuster Books for Young Readers, 2007. [bullying; GLBT]

Wittingler, Ellen. *What's in a Name.* New York: Simon & Schuster, 2000. [class; multiple cultural issues told in vignettes by multiple characters]

Wolf, Bernard. *Coming to America: A Muslim Family's Story.* New York: Lee & Low Books, 2003. [recent immigration]

Wong, Joyce Lee. *Seeing Emily.* New York: Amulet Books, 2005. [cultural conflict]

Yang, Gene Luen. *American Born Chinese.* New York: First Second, 2006. [cultural conflict; acceptance]

Zalben, Jane Breskin. *Unfinished Dreams.* New York: Simon & Schuster, 1996. [alienation; bullying; AIDS]

Zevin, Gabrielle. *Memoirs of a Teenage Amnesiac.* New York: Square Fish, 2007. [alienation]

Memoirs

Abeel, Samantha. *My Thirteenth Winter: A Memoir.* New York: Scholastic, 2003. [alienation-special needs]

Biederman, Alyssa. *My Rory: A Personal Journey through Teenage Anorexia.* New York, iUniverse, 2005. [body image]

Blanco, Jodee. *Please Stop Laughing at Me: One Woman's Inspirational True Story.* Avon, MA: Adams Media, 2010. [bullying]

Blanco, Jodee. *Please Stop Laughing at Us: One Survivor's Extraordinary Quest to Prevent School Bullying.* Dallas, TX: BenBella Books, 2008. [bullying]

Davis, Sampson, George Jenkins, and Rameck Hunt. *We Beat the Streets: How a Friendship Pact Led to Success.* New York: Dutton Children's Books, 2005. [self-respect]

Gottlieb, Lori. *Stick Figure: A Diary of My Former Self.* New York: Berkley Books, 2001. [body image]

Gruwell, Erin. *Freedom Writers' Diary: How a Teacher and 150 Teens Used Writing to Change Themselves and the World around Them.* With a foreword by Zlata Filipovic. New York: Broadway Books, 1999. [alienation; respect]

Hall, Megan Kelley and Carrie Jones, eds. *Dear Bully: 70 authors tell their stories.* New York: HarperTeen, 2011.

Hamilton, Bethany. *Soul Surfer: A True Story of Faith, Family, and Fighting to Get Back on the Board.* New York: Pocket Books, 2004. [alienation]

Jiménez, Francisco. *The Circuit Stories from the Life of a Migrant Child.* Albuquerque, NM: University of New Mexico Press, 1997. [contemporary immigration]

Myers, Walter Dean. *Bad Boy: A Memoir.* New York: HarperTempest, 2001. [alienation; self-esteem]

Parent, Lauren. *I'm Different But I'm Special.* Centennial, CO: Lifevest, 2006. [respect-special needs]

Rhodes-Courter, Ashley. *Three Little Words: A Memoir.* New York: Atheneum, 2008. [alienation]

Rodriguez, Diana Rodriguez. *Amor and Summer Secrets.* New York: Kensington, 2008. [culture conflict]

Rodriguez, Luis J. *Always Running: La Vida Loca: Gang Days in L.A.* New York: Simon & Schuster, 2005. [alienation; socioeconomic status; cultural conflict]

Santiago, Esmeralda. *When I Was Puerto Rican.* New York: Vintage Books, 1994. [recent immigration; cultural conflict]

Taylor, Blake E. S. *ADHD & Me: What I Learned from Lighting Fires at the Dinner Table.* With a foreword by Lara Honos-Webb. Oakland, CA: New Harbinger, 2007. [alienation; special needs]

Wheatley, Sharon. *'Til The Fat Girl Sings: From an Overweight Nobody to a Broadway Somebody—A Memoir.* Avon, MA: Adams Media, 2006. [body image]

Nonfiction Self-Help

Criswell, Patti. *Stand Up for Yourself and Your Friends: Dealing with Bullies and Bossiness and Finding a Better Way.* Middleton, WI: American Girl, 2009.

Davis, Brangien. *What's Real, What's Ideal: Overcoming a Negative Body Image*. Center City, MN: Hazelden Publishing & Educational Services, 1999.

Gumm, Merry L. *Help! I'm in Middle School . . . How Will I Survive?* Douglass, KS: NSR, 2004.

Humphrey, Sandra McLeod. *Hot Issues, Cool Choices: Facing Bullies, Peer Pressure, Popularity, and Put-Downs*. Amherst, New York: Prometheus Books, 2007.

Kaywell, Joan, ed. *Dear author: Letters of hope*. New York: Philomel Books, 2007.

Kaufman, Gershen, Lev Raphael, and Pamela Espeland. *Stick Up for Yourself: Every Kid's Guide to Personal Power and Positive Self-Esteem*. Minneapolis, MN: Free Spirit, 1999.

Kravetz, Jonathan. *How to Deal with Bullies*. New York: PowerKids, 2007.

Lock, James and Daniel Le Grange. *Help Your Teenager Beat an Eating Disorder*. New York: Guilford, 2005.

Slavens, Elaine. *Bullying: Deal with It Before Push Comes to Shove*. Toronto, ON: James Lorimer, 2010.

Periodicals

Current Health Kids. Weekly Reader Corporation.

Faces: People, Places, and Cultures. Carus Publishing.

National Geographic. National Geographic Society.

National Geographic Kids. National Geographic Society.

Skipping Stones: An International Multicultural Magazine. Skipping Stones.

Topics Online Magazine for Learners of English. http://www.topics-mag.com/index.html.

Books about Games

Barbarash, Lorraine. *Multicultural Games*. Champaign, IL: Human Kinetics, 1997.

Horowitz, Gayle L. *International Games: Building Skills through Multicultural Play*. Champaign, IL: Human Kinetics, 2009.

Lankford, Mary D, *Hopscotch around the World: Nineteen Ways to Play the Game*. New York: Beech Tree Books, 1992.

LeFevre, Dale N. *Best New Games: 77 Games and 7 Trust Activities for All Ages and Abilities*. Champaign, IL: Human Kinetics, 2002.

LeFevre, D Dale N. *The Spirit of Play: Cooperative Games for all Ages, Sizes, and Abilities*. Forres, Scotland: Findhorn, 2007.

Luvmour, Josette and Ba Luvmour. *Everyone Wins! Cooperative Games and Activities*. Gabriola Island, BC: New Society, 2007.

Ripoll, Oriol. *Play with Us: 100 Games from around the World*. Chicago: Chicago Review, 2005.

"Traditional Children's Games from around the World." *Topics Online Magazine*. http://www.topics-mag.com/internatl/traditional_games/section.htm.

9

ENDING THE YEAR WITH A FOCUS ON RESPECT

Students began the year noting similarities between themselves and other students and then took a step forward to valuing the importance of diversity. By the year's end, it is time to stress the importance of respecting everyone, not for what they can do, but for who they are. Classmates have seen how much they have in common, and they have noted how diversity adds to the collective. It is just as important at this time to understand the concept that everyone deserves respect, whether they are similar to us or not. And respect is due even when another person's contributions may not seem to complement or even enhance a collaborative venture.

In other words, there are no *others*. The "takeaway" at is point in the year for the students is that every person deserves respect just for being a human being. Rather than requiring that others perform "positively" to earn respect, the new perspective is that one can only *lose* respect by performing in negative ways.

END-OF-YEAR ACTIVITIES

After a year of seeing similarities and valuing diversity, the school year can be concluded with one or more synthesizing projects that "brings it all together" to ensure the idea of respect becomes memorable and enduring, to eliminate (or at least recognize) prejudices, and to allow students to value themselves. These activities may include the following sample culminating projects: a reading-writing venture, a multigenre endeavor, and a whole-team interdisciplinary artifact and poem.

MAKING THE ADOLESCENT LIFE MATTER: READING AND WRITING A BOOK

In his speech at the 2005 National Book Festival, Walter Dean Myers spoke about the characters in the books that adolescents want to read. He focused on the plight of the young people living in poverty in New Orleans. He emphasized the low graduation statistics of those entering eighth grade and pointed out that these adolescents, and those like them, are not apt to be included in our children's literature of today.

Mr. Myers argued that it is "important to include their lives in books . . . because they are humans." When he was a young man growing up in Harlem with parents who were laborers, he never saw himself in a book. And even at that young age, he was aware that books transmit values. "You go to school to learn who is valuable." Mr. Myers stressed that the way to make children feel part of our America is to bring them into literature.

Reading books in which adolescents see themselves reflected is important in any classroom. There are ways to integrate young adult literature in any content area. But even when not included in the curriculum, it is important to make these books accessible in middle school classrooms and libraries so that our children can see themselves and their communities in books, appreciate the temptations that are before them, and scrutinize the ways in which other adolescents (characters) handle these situations.

An extensive bibliography of picture books, poetry and short story collections, novels, memoirs, and nonfiction books that deal with the issues presented in these chapters—alienation, fitting in, relationships, bullying, and multiculturalism—is included in chapter 8.

While reading books about characters like oneself is constructive on many levels, even more empowering is writing a book in which the protagonist is based on oneself. While many students are not going to write a novel in middle school, a short work, such as a short story or poetry collection, a picture book, a short book or even a comic book, is achievable. Books that can be used as mentor texts are Sonya Sones's free-verse memoir *Stop Pretending*, Jeff Kinney's graphic *Diary of a Wimpy Kid*, and many of the picture books and short stories collections included in chapter 8.

Multigenre memoir collections encourage particularly strong writing and a sense of pride and illustrate that everyone has stories worth telling. Students can write about ages, objects, places, people, relationships, crises, and times of their lives.

Middle school students are not too old to hold an old-fashioned show-and-tell. The students bring in an object from the past that is of importance to them. This activity is held as part of a memoir writing and reading unit at the end of the year after community has been built and when students feel secure and respected enough to share what really mattered. While many students appear with baby blankets and stuffed animals—a surprise in itself—many bring artifacts from ancestors and relatives from divergent cultures. The students share the stories of their artifacts in small groups and are extremely respectful of each other's stories. This is why it is important to write about oneself only after students have built the trust and respect into their community, especially in middle school.

One year a student brought in his Fisher Price pirate ship. Quite a few of the other boys yelled out, "I had that," and surrounded him to play pirates for the next twenty minutes. They shared a culture and introduced it to the boys who had not had a Fisher Price childhood. As they shared their pirate stories, more and more memories came to light, and everyone had a memoir to write. The class continued this process, using music, poems, maps, photographs, picture books, and pictures to conjure up memories.

Norman Rockwell's iconic picture *The Discovery* is an illustration depicting a young child discovering a Santa suit in his father's dresser. Using the picture as a prompt in class typically leads to students' stories of finding out the Santa truth. But it also leads to sharing childhood crises that other students experienced in cultures that do not celebrate Christmas. All adolescents have valuable stories to tell and are the protagonists in these stories. For those students who are English language learners, their stories can be told in their native languages and then translated or told through drawings and pictures.

While this assignment is typically completed in language arts classes, there are interdisciplinary opportunities. Illustrations can be added in art class; photographs and other artwork, even movie clips, in technology class; statistics can be examined in math; and the effects of environment in science and national and local events in social studies. Another way to include an autobiographical writing of this type in science class or social studies is for students to place themselves in an environment, time period, or event being studied.

Humanities students wrote *You Were There* books about the Holocaust (Roessing 2007b). One student featured herself as the "You" in the event as she took herself back in time to a World War II concentration camp. In this way, she was able to examine her feelings and reactions to a situation that other adolescents went through at a different time and place. Following this model, the teacher poses the question, "How would *you* react to living in the desert, in 1840, in China?" When the classroom contains a library of books written about *us*, every student truly "feels part of America [or our school]," and as Walter Dean Myers indicated, this is a demonstration of respect.

UBUNTU PROJECT

One year, as the class finished Sheila Gordon's novel about apartheid in South Africa, *Waiting for the Rain*. An editorial by Jim Carnes (1997, 4), printed in the *Teaching Tolerance* magazine, introduced the African concept *ubuntu*. Mr. Carnes explained,

> *Ubuntu*, from the Nguni language, is one of those well-loved, elemental words that defy simple translation. The closest English equivalent is 'humaneness,' or 'the quality of being human.' A proverb common across Africa expresses the ubuntu ideal: 'A person is a person through other people.'

Carnes quotes from a justice of the Constitutional Court of South Africa who explained the concept as follows:

> [Ubuntu] is a culture which places some emphasis on communality and on the interdependence of the members of a community. It recognizes a person's status as a human being, entitled to unconditional respect, dignity, value and acceptance from the members of the community such person happens to be part of. It also entails the converse, however. The person has a corresponding duty to give the same respect, dignity, value and acceptance to each member of that community.

An *ubuntu* project focusing on respect seemed an effective way to end a yearlong study of tolerance and human rights. The students were aware that less than ten years after the events depicted in *Waiting for the Rain*, South Africa held its first all-race election. Apartheid officially ended, and a new constitution was adopted. Jim Carnes observed that *ubuntu*, the ancient African concept, was enshrined in that new constitution.

The students were asked to examine this notion and share their insights and interpretation of *ubuntu*. The result was the Ubuntu Project:

The Ubuntu Project

This year we have been studying literature that deals, on some level, with the concept of *ubuntu*. Keep in mind the problems and ideas encountered in *The Diary of Anne Frank*, "Flowers for Algernon," *Haroun and the Sea of Stories*, *I Heard the Owl Call My Name*, and *Waiting for the Rain*, as well as Shakespeare's *Much Ado About Nothing* and many of our short stories and poetry.

- Demonstrate *your* understanding of *ubuntu*. Show examples from history, from the world today, or from a concept, hope, or dream in your mind.
- Use a medium (expression) other than essay or informational writing format—music, song, drama, poetry, drawing, painting, graphics, sculpture, photography, collage, scrapbook, or newspaper made up of authentic news articles. You are limited only by your own imagination. When choosing a medium, keep your particular talents and interests in mind.
- There is no correct or incorrect response as long as you communicate your understanding or vision of *ubuntu*.

Be creative. Take a risk. Try something new. Use your own special talents.

Respect for the students was demonstrated by letting them create their own projects. The only requirements were that they be ready to present their project on the due date and that they verbally introduce their project with an explanation of their interpretation and their decision on the medium in which they were presenting. The work was to be done outside of class, and all students kept journals of their thinking, their decisions, and their process. They were permitted to use any materials from the classroom as well as any outside resources they might provide on their own.

That first year, students presented during class periods to their classmates. There were quite a variety of projects that promoted a diversity of talent. Some of the aptitudes demonstrated surprised everyone. Students felt free to tap into their creativity for three reasons: no one else was dependent on the outcome; they had invested a year getting to know each other, seeing similarities, and valuing diversity; and there was no right or wrong answer. The project was a matter of personal interpretation and choice. Some of the presentation formats were more conventional, but many were completely unexpected:

- A quilt; each square had a symbol of *ubuntu* explained in a narration.
- A photographic essay.
- Trading cards of *ubuntu* heroes that each contained an explanation of how the acts of heroism exhibited "ubuntu-ness."
- A newspaper composed of articles and cartoons garnered from newspapers, each one followed by an explanation of why it was included.
- An original dance composition and performance.
- A skit.
- A materials and picture collage.
- A video essay.
- A song collage.
- A video collage.
- Original artwork.
- An interactive exhibit.
- An original clay sculpture.
- An exhibit integrating cultural quotations and an original poem.
- An original poem:

My Pathway by Brian E.

I have strolled the gnarled pathway of a long and difficult life,
And as I lie here resting, I recall everyone who has made it bright.
In these people's faces I saw nothing but agony and despair,
But I was sure, if I looked hard, there was more to be seen there.
They taught me and helped me when I lost my sense
And comforted me when I was tense.
 If there was one thing about these people that I could sustain
 Was their silent urge to be humane.

I was a boy; he was my dad;
I can remember all the fun that we had.
He gladly took me to the park
And comforted me when I was afraid of the dark.
He set a good example by being kind
And helped me straighten out thoughts in my mind.
 If there was one thing about this man that I could sustain
 Was his silent urge to be humane.

I was a teen; he was my friend.
I called him *John*; he called me *Ken*.
One day he said, "We're best friends, me and you."
I replied, "Yeah, I know. You're my buddy too."
He bought me things because I was poor,
But I never, ever asked for more.
 If there is one thing about this youth that I could sustain
 Was this silent urge to be humane.

I was a man; she was my wife.
We'd be together for the rest of our life.
After dinner one night she whispered,
"I love you," and when I kissed her,
It made me feel as if we'd never part;
On a long, twisting journey we would embark.
 If there is one thing about this woman that I could sustain
 Was her silent urge to be humane.

I was old; she was a stranger;
She was different, but I'd never change her.
She fell down; I helped her up;
I gave her tea, warm in a cup.

She was cold, so I gave her my coat.
With watery eyes, she turned and she wrote:
   "You have been wonderful; you've been great.
   But I feel for me it is a bit too late.
   Do not miss me when I am gone,
   For I truly do not wish to live on.
   I wish there were more people just like you;
   More people to do the things that you do.
   If there was one thing about you, sir, that I could sustain
   Is your silent urge to be humane."

The class concluded the project as reflective thinkers (see Ubuntu Project Self-Appraisal).

In the following years, the Ubuntu Project presentations were held in the evening so that family and friends could attend. In addition to some of the formats used the prior year, such as collages and sculptures, there were some especially creative presentations: a movie titled *What Makes Us Human?*; two *ubuntu* board games; an original song—lyrics and music; a candle sculpture; and *A Perfect World*, a picture book.

The most unique project may have been the paper-cutting project. Brigette used the Chinese art form in which all the intricate cuts are made internally with a knife or small scissors. She designed and cut a tree formed from people. Her accompanying journal expressed a journey of emotional peaks and valleys as she led the reader through days of blisters and bleeding fingers, only to find the whole process worthwhile when her mother and sister bought her a frame for her project. Her journal entry ended with her visualizing her artwork over the fireplace of her "future first home." There are not many projects that are so memorable.

The Ubuntu Project continued to spark more creative expressions in following years with paintings, plays, video games, drawings, and, in 2002, "Ubuntu Moem," a movie poem!

The Ubuntu Project was effective, not because of the project itself, but because the assignment required adolescents to think about respect and humaneness and to interpret those concepts in their own unique ways. More often we hear about "earning respect" rather than being owed respect just for being a human being, being only responsible for not losing that privilege.

Ubuntu Project Self-Appraisal

Take me through your month with *ubuntu* from the moment you received the assignment sheet until the moment you finished your presentation. The questions should be integrated into, and covered by, your journal entries.

I.   Thinking/Planning
     Interpretation: What went through your mind as you searched, chose, rejected, chose your personal interpretation of *ubuntu*?
     Format: Once you decided on an interpretation, how did you determine your presentation format? What went through your mind and heart as you went through the process of choosing (rejecting and rechoosing)? On what did you base your decisions? Did you begin in any other directions, and what made you change directions? How much time was spent in the thinking (brainstorming) and planning (organizing) stage?
II. Working/Construction of the Project:
     Describe your *time* commitment, your working time. How much time was spent in the actual construction of the project? How did you go about the *creation* of your project?
III. Presentation
     What time and effort was spent on the planning of the actual in-front-of-the-class presentation? How did you practice?
     Describe your views and feelings about your actual presentation.
IV. Evaluation: Appraise your Project
     Concept
     Amount of Work
     Effort (mental and physical)
     Communication
     Creativity
     Commitment
     Of what were you most proud? What would you change, add, or delete?

The effectiveness of this assignment became apparent when three girls from the class became furious with one of their classmates. It seemed that classmates had made a comment about another student that the others felt revealed a lack of tolerance and respect, and "It was after Ubuntu!" they cried, outraged.

Although this assignment fits well within a humanities curriculum, it is also the type of year-end project that can be assigned as an interdisciplinary team endeavor. Some teams have talent shows or academic fairs based on respect, as the topic could cross content area boundaries and share talent.

LEAVING A LEGACY

A class should leave a lasting positive imprint on the school. A capstone project, one that symbolizes the students' similarities and diversity and their respect for both, may be an appropriate eighth grade activity, completed before the students leave middle school. Students may collaboratively design and create a work of art for the school—a mural, collage, or mosaic, something to which everyone can contribute in some way. Such a project would easily involve all the content area classes: in science class students would investigate materials that would adhere the best and substances that would combine well and complement each other, in mathematics class students would plan the dimensions and scale models, in social studies class students would plan the scene(s) in a current social context, and in art class, of course, students would create the artifact. This may be the one activity that does not lean heavily on language arts, although the students could compose a prose or poetry narration to accompany the artwork or for an inauguration presentation to the school. A mosaic, collage, or mural of scenes also lends itself to working collaboratively while valuing the diversity of individuals as each student designs his or her tile, section, or "piece of the puzzle."

The class mosaic—whether a traditional tile mosaic, a painted mural, a cloth quilt, or a collage of materials, like a metaphor—further conveys each student's integral role in the class and is an iconic record for the future.

COMING FULL CIRCLE: MANY VOICES, ONE VERSE

The year began with "I Am" poems and even a "We Are" poem, poems that were about the individuals who make up the class. At the conclusion of the year, each class, or the team as a whole, is able to compose genuine "We Are" poetry, writing about the group as a whole, rather than the individual students. The poems become interdisciplinary work as they add elements from each of their content area classes:

We are . . . the _____ Team of _____ Middle School.

We wonder . . . what high school will be like—will we find our classrooms, be prepared?

We hear . . . the cannons fire as the Union wins the Battle of Gettysburg.

We see . . . our classmates' hair stand on end when we study static electricity.

We want . . . our algebraic equations to balance.

We are . . . learning how to think and write like scientists as we hypothesize, test, and analyze.

We pretend . . . that we are the textile workers of Lowell, Massachusetts, fighting for labor reform, and in language arts

We feel . . . sorry for the victims of the Holocaust and tell their stories through our poetry.

We touch . . . the clay in art class and make sculptures that sit in the school "museum."

We worry . . . about forgetting all the comma rules and using them in our essays.

We try . . . to be prepared for the state standardized tests.

We are . . . studying chemistry, physics, algebra, the Civil War and Industrial Revolution, many cultures, and *The Diary of Anne Frank* in our eighth-grade curriculum.

We understand . . . from health classes that we need to eat from the food groups and exercise regularly to live long, productive lives.

We say . . . *Bon Jour, Guten Tag, and Buenos Dias* as we study French, German, and Spanish while

We dream . . . that we travel to all the countries and cultures we study
in Around-the-World class.

We try . . . to build our stamina to run the mile for the Presidential
Fitness Award;

We hope . . . we are prepared for high school and will find a group to
which we belong like this year because

We are . . . the _____ Team of _____ Middle School, and we know
each other well.

Through these relics—the books, the presentations, the artifacts, and
the poem—all the children have become a part of the same culture, that
of their team, their school, and their community; and in that way, we
are preparing them to become citizens of their world. "You go to school
to learn who is valuable" (Myers 2005). We succeed when each student
respects, not only that he or she is valuable, but that we all are.

APPENDIX: LESSONS AND ACTIVITIES BY CONTENT AREAS

REFERENCES

Abbott, Edwin A. 2005. *Flatland: A Romance of Many Dimensions.* Amherst, NY: Prometheus Books.

Allport, Gordon W. 1976. "Prejudice and the Individual." In *The Black American Reference Book*, edited by Marbel M. Smythe, 515–21. Englewood Cliffs, NJ: Prentice-Hall.

Allport, Gordon W. 1979. *The Nature of Prejudice.* Reading, MA: Addison-Wesley.

Angelou, Maya. 1993. *Wouldn't take nothing for my journey now.* New York: Bantam Books.

"American Renaissance. Kids stay separate outside of class." (n.d.) Reproduction of the article "50 years after Brown vs. Board of Ed, school cafeterias still divided" by T. Mask and M. George, March 9, 2004. *Detroit Free Press.* Retrieved from http://www.amren.com/news/news04/02/26/segregation.html

Carnes, Jim. 1997. "The age of Ubuntu." *Teaching Tolerance* 12.

Coloroso, Barbara. 2011. "Bully, Bullied, Bystander . . . and Beyond. Help Your Students Choose a New Role." *Teaching Tolerance* 39, 51–53.

Davis, Stan and Charisse Nixon. 2010. Preliminary results from the Youth Voice research project: Victimization & strategies. www.youthvoiceproject.com/YVPMarch2010.pdf.

Fleischman, Paul. 1988. *Joyful Noise: Poems for Two Voices.* New York: Harper-Collins.

Fluegelman, Andrew. 1976. *The New Games Book: Play Hard, Play Fair, Nobody Hurt*. New York: Doubleday.

Fox, Mem. 1989. *Feathers and Fools*. San Diego: Voyager Books.

Fox, Charles and Norman Gimbel. 1973. "I got a name," recorded by Jim Croce. *I got a name*. New York: ABC Records. LP album.

Gardner, Howard. 2004. *Frames of Mind. The Theory of Multiple Intelligences*. New York: Basic Books.

George, Marshall A. 2002. "Living on the Edge: Confronting Social Injustices." *Voices from the Middle* 9 (5): 39–44.

Gordon, Shelia. 1989. *Waiting for the Rain*. London: Starfire.

Handlin, Oscar. 1964. *Out of Many: A Study Guide to Cultural Pluralism in the United States*. New York: Anti-Defamation League of B'nai B'rith.

———. 1986. "America: a world of difference." In *A World of Difference: Teacher/Student Resource Guide*. New York: Anti-Defamation League of B'nai B'rith.

Hughes, Langston. 1994. "I, Too, Sing America." In *The collected poems of Langston Hughes*, edited by Langston Hughes, Arnold Rampersad, and David Roessel.

Humphrey, Hubert. 1967. "All-America tribute to Archbishop Iakovos." Speech presented in Chicago, Illinois

"The 'In' Crowd and Social Cruelty with John Stossel." 2002. ABC News Special. New York: American Broadcasting Corporation.

Jackson, Alan. 2007. "Where I Come From." *Greatest Hits 2*. Nashville: Arista. Audio CD.

Johnson, David W. and Roger T. Johnson. 2000. "The Three Cs of Reducing Prejudice and Discrimination." In *Reducing Prejudice and Discrimination*, edited by Stuart Oskamp, 239–68. Mahwah, NJ: Lawrence Erlbaum.

Kinney, Jeff. 2007. *Diary of a Wimpy Kid*. New York: Amulet Books.

Leff, Stephen and Munro, J. 2009. "Bully-Proofing Playgrounds During School Recess." http://www.education.com/reference/article/promoting-social -skills-prevent-bullying/.

Lowry, Lois. 1993. *The Giver*. New York: Dell-Laurel Leaf.

Lyon, George Ella. 1999. *Where I'm From, Where Poems Come From*. Spring, TX: Absey.

Mask, Teresa and Maryanne George. 2004. "Kids Stay Separate Outside of Class: They Prefer Comfort to Integration; That's OK, the Experts Say." *Detroit Free Press*, February 25.

McAnally, Mac. 1996. "Back Where I Come From." *Me and You*, recorded by Kenny Chesney. Nashville: BNA Entertainment. Album.

Myers, Walter Dean. September 24, 2005. Webcast. Book Fest 2005. Library of Congress. http://www.loc.gov/today/cyberlc/feature_wdesc.php?rec=3762#.

National Council for the Social Studies. 2012. Accessed February 27, 2011. http://www.socialstudies.org/about.

Pettigrew, Thomas F. 1998. "Intergroup Contact Theory." *Annual Review of Psychology* 49: 65–85.

Portnoy, Gary and Judy Hart Angello. 2003. "Theme from Cheers." *Keeper*. Toronto, ON: Argentum.

Robbins, Tom. 2003. *Skinny legs and all*. New York: Bantam Books.

Rockwell, Norman. 1956. *The Discovery*. Cover illustration for *The Saturday Evening Post*, December 29, 1956, retrieved from http://arthistory.about .com/od/from_exhibitions/ig/american_chronicles/aonr_dia_09_17.htm

Rodgers, Richard and Oscar Hammerstein II. 2000. "Getting to Know You." On *The King and I*, recorded by Gertrude Lawrence. Paris, France: Decca Broadway. Audio CD.

Roessing, Lesley. 2004. "Building a Community of Stories and Writers: Lake Wobegon Comes to the Classroom." *Quarterly* 26 (4): 18–24.

———. 2005. "Creating Empathetic Connections to Literature." *Quarterly* 27 (2): 7–11, 28.

———. 2006. "What's in a Name? A Whole Lot of Talking, Researching, and Writing." *Voices from the Middle* 14 (2): 22–30.

———. 2007a. "Making Connections: The Home Front Fair." *Middle Ground* 10 (4): 32–33.

———. 2007b. "Making Research Matter." *English Journal* 96 (4): 50–55.

———. 2009. *The Write to Read: Response Journals That Increase Comprehension*. Thousand Oaks, CA: Corwin.

Romano, Carlin. 2011. "Us vs. Them: Good News from the Ancients." *Chronicle of Higher Education* 57(21): B5–B6.

Rylant, Cynthia. 1982. *When I Was Young in the Mountains*. New York: Dutton Children's Books.

Sheff, David. 2010. *All We Are Saying: The Last Major Interview with John Lennon and Yoko Ono*, New York: St. Martin's.

Santiago, Esmeralda. 1994. *When I Was Puerto Rican*. New York: Vintage Books.

Sones, Sonya. 2001. *Stop Pretending: What Happened When My Big Sister Went Crazy*. New York: HarperTeen.

Sugarland, with Kristian Bush, Kristen Hall, and Jennifer Nettles. 2004a. "Hello." *Twice the Speed of Life*. Nashville: Mercury Nashville. Audio CD.

Sugarland, with Kristian Bush, Kristen Hall, and Jennifer Nettles. 2004b. "Small Town Jericho." *Twice the Speed of Life*. Nashville: Mercury Nashville. Audio CD.

Whitman, Walt. 2004. *Leaves of Grass*. New York: Bantam Dell.

ABOUT THE AUTHOR

Lesley Roessing taught middle school for over twenty years in suburban Philadelphia, Pennsylvania. She has written articles for NCTE's *English Journal* and *Voices from the Middle*; the *Quarterly*, a NWP publication; and AMLE's *Middle School Journal* and *Middle Ground*. Her book on reader response, *The Write to Read: Response Journals That Increase Comprehension*, was published in 2009.

In addition, Roessing has presented her strategies and ideas widely in a variety of formats—from state, national, and international conferences of teachers' associations to workshops for organizations and schools across the country. In the fall of 2009, Ms. Roessing moved to South Carolina to serve as director of the Coastal Savanna Writing Project and as instructor of adolescent education at Armstrong Atlantic State University in Savannah, Georgia, where she works with teachers and students.

Made in the USA
Monee, IL
08 January 2020